Dr. Albert Zehr's

Healthy
Steps

to Maintain or Regain Natural Good Health

Albert Zehr, Ph.D.

Abundant Health Publishers • Burnaby, Canada

This book is intended to be informational and educational. It should not be used to diagnose or treat disease. The programs presented are recommendations, not prescriptions. When needing treatment, please consult a medical professional who is familiar with nutritional therapy. Neither the author nor the publisher authorize the use of any material contained in this book in connection with the promotion of any product.

HEALTHY STEPS to Maintain or Regain Natural Good Health

Published in Canada by Abundant Health Publishers
Cover Design by Caleb Chang
Printed in Canada

Canadian Cataloguing in Publication Data

Zehr, Albert, 1938-
  Healthy steps to maintain or regain
natural good health

  ISBN 0-9694418-0-0

  1. Health. 2. Diet in disease. 3.
Dietary supplements. I. Title.
Ra776.5.Z44 1990   613   C90-091105-0

ACKNOWLEDGEMENTS

This book is really a family affair.

To son Ron who spent numerous hours in editing, design, layout and publication.

To daughter Sheryl who researched the herb chapters, and did computer input.

To daughter Janelle, our resident artist, who created all of the art work.

To daughter Marilyn, our most patient "guinea pig," who allows Dad to try all of his "stuff" on her.

And to wife Janet who knows me best, yet still supports and trusts me, and believes in what I have to say.

THANKS DEAR FAMILY from Dad who has the ideas, but could never make it alone.

Contents

How to Use this Book

Chapters 1-3: Basic Philosophy of Natural Good Health
>In other words, where is the writer coming from? Why does he think we get sick? What makes him think that he has the answers? Do not miss this section.

Chapters 4-11: Specific Programs for Particular Needs
>These chapters present a simple analysis and explanation of particular health problems and present nutritional programs to help the body overcome each problem. Notice the introductory comments, the brief summary of what the chapter contains, the testimonials of some who have been helped, and then a clear understandable description of the problem, followed by the suggested program.
>
>A dagger (†) after a suggested supplement indicates that a detailed formula appears in Appendix C. Specific quantities are suggestions only. If that potency is not available, use something close to it.

Chapters 12-14: Herbs and Clay
>These chapters examine traditional uses of selected herbs, herbal combinations and clay.

Reference Material
>The appendices contain handy reference charts showing health problems and commonly suggested herbs and vitamins. Here, you will also find more detailed formulas for the multi-nutrient supplements recommended in certain programs. Finally, there is a list of books recommended to provide additional information.

While this book may be valuable to read through, it has the potential to be an invaluable reference to lead the serious reader step by step to maintain or to regain natural good health.

Introduction

Science, technology, medicine, and the knowledge explosion seem to spell progress in every area of modern society. Yet, behind the scenes of apparent progress, we find an ever increasing amount of sickness, disease, ill health, fatigue, hospitalization, heart disease, cancer, and medical side effects.

As to human health, Dr. Zehr feels that we need to come back, back to the simple basic facts; back to working with our bodies, rather than against them; and back to cooperating with our bodies' defenses, rather than frustrating and harassing them.

While the Nineties promise to be a decade marked by concern for the environment, Dr. Zehr suggests that that concern should be mirrored by an equal concern for our inner environment, as he calls it the *invironment*. As the abuse of the environment destroys the world's ecological balance and bodes disaster for the future, even so the abuse of our "invironment" destroys our body's biological balance and promises sickness and disease.

In the following pages, we find not only a sound and basic logic to help the reader understand why many people get caught in the sickness syndrome, but also basic and workable steps to follow in striding toward natural good health.

The first two chapters present clear and basic logic to help the reader understand why so many people get caught in the sickness syndrome. The simple yet profound truth of how we can release our bodies' determination and ability to be well, and even to regain vibrant health after sickness has struck, dawns clear in chapter two. Chapter three not only makes good nutrition both clear and logical, but also gives the reader a solid plan for optimum nutrition with a carefully researched supplement program.

Body cleansing, detoxification, and colon cleansing are explained and illustrated in chapter four. A comprehensive fourteen day body cleansing program is described in detail.

The following five chapters give a clear and understandable explanation of a number of health complications. Immune weak-

3

ness, Candida Albicans yeast disease, overweight, heart disease, and Chronic Fatigue Syndrome (also known as Epsein-Barr virus syndrome, or Myalgic Encephalomeylitis) are all described and natural programs to help the body deal with these problems are presented in the following chapters.

Some basic secrets about resting and sleeping naturally, and maintaining natural good memory and mental alertness are revealed along with suggestions for supplement intake to facilitate these natural processes.

The final chapters touch yet another area which is very important for helping yourself to better health. Herbs and clay, the original medicines, have been used in healing since the beginning. Their effectiveness is so amazing that they have frequently been overlooked largely because the results obtained often cannot be explained or understood. Of course, when considering natural good health, understanding is really secondary. Enjoying it the way it was meant to be is of primary importance.

Thousands have walked out of many different health problems by following the steps outlined herein. It is our sincere hope that many more, by reading and following the pathways clearly pointed out in this book, will be enabled to join forces with their bodies to march out of health breakdown and on toward natural good health.

Chapter 1

Backward Steps Toward Ill Health

Your health may be in trouble before you even know it. An ever-increasing number of North Americans are plodding steadily backward toward ill health. Every year their aches and pains increase and health breakdown continues. Even more serious is the fact that the "help" often available frequently compounds the problem and speeds up the downward pace.

In this chapter you will discover:

• What is the natural state of the human body.

• Why health breakdown is inevitable for most people.

• What are six great frustrators to good health.

• How good health is destroyed by typical lifestyle.

It is estimated that today over thirty percent of hospital patients are in hospitals because of medications, surgeries and other forms of "doctoring." The help they had trusted to give them relief, having ignored the body's natural functions, breaks down rather than builds up their health. Iatrogenic or "doctor-caused" disease is becoming a major problem in countries with "advanced" medical establishments. In fact, it has been estimated that each year more people are killed by prescription drugs than by accidents on the road!

If someone else is expected to bring us out of trouble, it is not important for us to know how we got to where we are. But, if we are going to get ourselves out of trouble, then we must know how we came to be in such a state.

Although we may not be entirely and solely responsible for our health breakdown, it will certainly have to be we ourselves who take responsibility to get out of it. In order to do this, it is important to know how we got where we now are.

The human body was made to be healthy; it desires to be healthy; and if it is not healthy, it will do everything it can to return to good health. It follows then that if it is not well, there must be some reason. In order to understand how to get well, it is helpful to see how and why our health breaks down.

Under present conditions, our bodies are often undernourished, and bombarded with pollutants in air, water and food. While we feed on fat-laden, over-processed empty calorie foods, our toxin-loaded system gets neither adequate exercise nor proper elimination. This places extra stress on a poorly supplied system and breakdown becomes inevitable.

The Great Frustrators

Let us take some time to consider six great frustrators which work to drag us backward to ill health. Five are white and one is black. Besides all the obvious factors like chemicals, pollution and stress, it seems that these six elements lie behind more ill health than any others.

1) White Sugar

The human body was not made with the capacity to deal with sugar or refined carbohydrates. Many foods, especially fruits, contain natural sugars which we refer to as complex carbohydrates. While these can be processed by the body, taking in pure sugar is like putting a very highly refined, high-octane fuel into a diesel engine. The fuel, burning much hotter than the engine was made for, would soon cause burnout and breakdown. In addition, sugar, being highly refined, has been stripped of its nutrients and therefore supplies empty calories which put further stress on the body's metabolism. Diabetes, hypoglycemia, and obesity afflict millions. An increase in sugar intake in society is matched by an increase in these diseases; yet though they are clearly due to excess sugar intake, sugar continues to be added to virtually every processed food on the market shelf.

2) White Salt

Salt was used historically to preserve foods and to make putrid meat more palatable. It is no longer needed for either of these reasons, yet it is still used habitually. Consider the following five reasons for throwing away your salt shaker:

First, sodium chloride is an inorganic chemical and is of no value as a food. The arctic discoverer, Stefansson, noted that the Eskimos got along very well without it. He further learned that if one does without it for three months, the desire for salt disappears.

Second, table salt contains no vitamins or organic minerals and cannot be digested or assimilated.

Third, salt is harmful to the heart, and may be a major factor in causing high blood pressure and hardening of the arteries.

Fourth, it places great stress on the kidneys, may cause damage and be involved in kidney breakdown and disease.

Fifth, it replaces calcium and potassium in the body, which may lead to osteoporosis and heart disease.

While more could be said, it is already clear that salt does not work with the body, but very much against it. The sensation that salt brings added flavor should disappear after salt has not been used for several months.

3) White Flour

Take beautiful whole grain and strip it of the fiber which the body needs for proper bowel function. Then, rob it of the life germ and the endosperm which contain vitamins, minerals and protein. Next, apply chlorine dioxide gas to bleach what remains. Now that it looks beautifully white, is insect proof (Insects cannot survive on it!), and has an indefinite shelf-life, sell it to every baker in the land and let them bake lifeless bread to form the main staple of the nation's diet. Oh, by the way, since the flour has been robbed of its wealth and natural riches, add a trace of synthetic vitamins and call it "enriched." In case you are not yet convinced, here is one more point to consider: white flour is more effective as a wallpaper paste than as a food.

Do your health a favor — eat only whole grains, and choose a variety instead of wheat alone.

4) Milk

This one may be more controversial. Here are a number of reasons why it is better not to drink milk.

First, your mother was not a cow. No other creature on earth drinks the milk of another species. Each species produces milk in order to meet the unique needs of its offspring.

Second, pasteurization destroys up to two-thirds of the vitamins and minerals and ninety per cent of the enzymes. It also causes alterations in the fatty acids and the protein.

Third, homogenization occurs when the milk is forced by pressure against steel. This process breaks up the fat molecules so that the butterfat no longer rises to the top. Once the fat molecules are broken, they can easily pass through the gut wall. This may allow an excess amount of fat to enter the bloodstream and thus contribute to heart disease.

Fourth, antibiotics such as penicillin and other medications given to cattle are passed on to their milk, and become a part of this popular beverage.

If one still wishes to drink milk, it is better to drink pure, raw, fresh, unpasteurized milk and in small quantities. Observation and experience have convinced me that milk is not nearly as healthy or as essential as advertisements have led us to believe. Children in other countries who do not drink milk are not less healthy. Recently, an Asian family asked me why their ten-year-old son had so many mucus, allergy, and asthma type reactions. I suggested that they stop giving him milk. The mother suddenly remembered that when they had visited Taiwan and could not find milk for him, he had been much better.

5) Cigarettes

By now, what the "health nuts" have been saying for years has been proven by science and medicine and by the millions who gave up their lives for the great pleasure of smoking. Statistics show that the equivalent of one jumbo jet load of people die daily from smoking-induced illnesses. From this, we can certainly conclude that smoking makes about as much sense as getting onto a jumbo jet that probably has a bomb on it!

6) Coffee

While coffee contains no nutrients, it does contain an active drug, caffeine. Besides being addictive, this drug can raise blood pressure, increase pulse rate, stimulate the kidneys and temporarily relieve fatigue or depression. While these actions may seem minor, it can eventually be a contributing factor to the development of related disease.

Caffeine sensitivity has been linked to breast lumps. Accord-

ing to Jonathon V. Wright M.D., in *Healing With Nutrition,* "Caffeine elimination has received remarkably widespread publicity as one means of treating cystic mastitis or fibrocystic heart disease. For many women, stopping all coffee, tea, chocolate, cocoa, and caffeine containing colas and medications is so effective that no other measures are needed."

Caffeine has also been shown to cause

twice as much calcium to be excreted from the body as is normal.

While it may be argued whether or not the above factors actually cause certain diseases, there is no doubt that they can begin the health breakdown syndrome. The body being frustrated by these factors expresses itself in a symptomatic way. The headache, pain, itch or other symptom is treated with some form of chemical to suppress the symptomatic expression. While the symptom may be suppressed, more stress is put on the body, and further breakdown is almost inevitable. Since we are concerned not only with how to get out of a breakdown, but also with how to avoid it, we would do well to avoid these six factors.

Modern Lifestyle

Consider the following scenario. John E. Average rises with only enough time for a donut (fiberless, vitamin-robbed white flour and refined carbohydrate "empty calorie" sugar) and coffee (polluted water, caffeine, high-fat cream, and more lifeless sugar) served in a ceramic mug that may well be leaching lead.

At breaktime he grabs a soft drink and sweet roll with more of the above ingredients. This again sends his blood sugar sky high, until his exhausted pancreas can muster up a panic load of insulin. The insulin is more than his body needs, and in an hour John feels blah again!

At noon there is only time to head for a drive-through fast food restaurant (no exercise), wait in the line surrounded by car exhaust (pollution), and snatch a burger (grease, fat) on a white bun (lifeless bleached white flour) loaded with mayonnaise (more fat, sugar, additives, and preservatives) and fries (fat, grease) and cola (more empty calories and caffeine).

Afternoon snack is more of the above. By dinner time he has little energy, so he pops a few TV dinners (hormone-fed beef and gravy, or mercury-spiked fish, with white flour noodles and twice-cooked vegetables all packaged in aluminum foil) into the oven.

After dinner John drives through "smog city" to pick up a friend at the airport. While at the airport he contacts the viruses and germs from 20 nations. His friend has a bad cold which he picked up somewhere abroad.

At bedtime John takes a painkiller for his headache and a laxative for constipation and writes a reminder to call his doctor to see if he can get some antibiotics for his recurring sore throat.

The above is an abridged one-act play called "Modern Living." As this "lifestyle" continues, the body begins to express its inner breakdown by external symptoms. Headache, rash, pain, stiffness, itching, swelling, bloating, stomach-ache, and so forth are all symptoms of inner distress. Because consumers demand symptomatic relief, drugs and medications have been produced to short circuit and suppress the body's ability to express itself symptomatically. Besides ignoring the real problem, these drugs further pollute and stress the body and set the stage for deeper and more serious problems in the future.

The body's immune system which is so vital in defending and protecting the body from foreign invasion (see chapter 5), already overworked, is frustrated and overwhelmed by this deliberate chemical attack. The body's crucial elimination and cleansing activities are frustrated by a lack of dietary fiber and daily exercise, and are already carrying a backlog of debris. Therefore, there is no reserve capacity to cleanse the system adequately (see chapter 4); hence, the toxicity accumulates. Chronic ill health is becoming more inevitable as each day passes.

The above is just a sketch and perhaps an over-simplification, but should serve to give us a clear realization of the dilemma so many are facing. Hopefully it has also helped to prepare us for our journey as we take the following HEALTHY STEPS toward natural good health.

Chapter 2

Getting in Step with Our Body

Our body was made to be well. Its constant desire and continuous effort is always geared toward being well. Should it not be well, it has an amazing capacity to restore and even heal itself. With such a force on our side, it should be very unusual for us to be ill, and in fact, it is true that disease and sickness are abnormal. Therefore, it follows that if we would fully cooperate and join forces with our bodies, sickness should rarely occur. If it does occur, we should be able to walk out of it by understanding and following the four principles outlined in this chapter.

In this chapter you will discover:

• What are the natural steps toward good health.

• How the body has an innate desire to move toward good health.

• What you can do to help your child take the first steps toward good health.

It's Natural to be Healthy

At the moment an infant is born, that small body contains all the organs and "equipment" that it will ever contain. Of course, the organs are still in an undeveloped and immature form. The full development depends entirely on air, food and water. Provided the child is normal, proper quality and adequate supply of these three necessities should maintain good health and produce a mature adult without sickness or disease. In other words, good health is not a matter of being lucky or of being born to a doctor, but rather it is the normal and natural consequence of being what we all were meant to be.

If it is that simple, then why is everyone sick? When we understand the answer to this question, we will be more able not only to avoid but also to overcome sickness. Why is everyone sick? The answer to this question is simple: people are not in step with their bodies.

Now, let us go back to our little infant. We shall call him "Abner" and follow his history to see why such a perfect specimen of humanity could ever be sick.

The First Principle: Maintaining the Breath of Life

At the very moment of his birth, Abner's first impulse is to breathe air. This first reaction sets the constant and basic require-ment for fresh, clean air, a substance which will always be neces-sary for good health. A lack of air, poor quality air, or contaminated air may violate this first principle. This violation may cause break-down and disease. This being the case, we must work with the body and assure ourselves clean, fresh air.

Oxygen is the life factor in air and must always be freely available if ideal human health is to be maintained. Every cell in the body needs a constant supply of oxygen. The damage caused by a stroke or heart attack is primarily a result of an interruption in the supply of oxygen.

Consider the abuses of the first principle that Abner will see all around him as he grows up. Besides poor breathing habits such as shallow breathing, we breathe fumes at work and on the

15

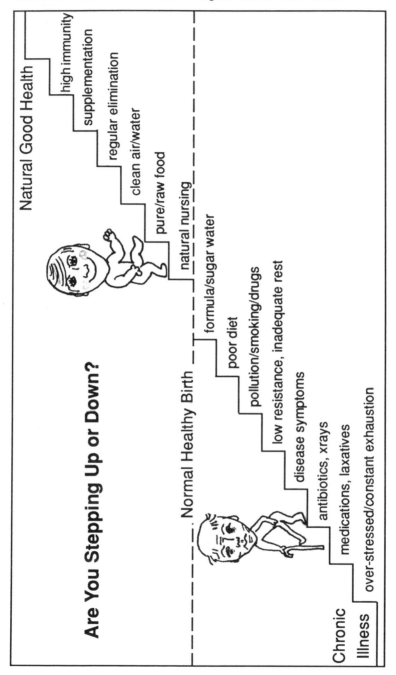

road. As if this were not enough, we deliberately inhale carcino-
genic tar and nicotine into our lungs to give ourselves a fleeting
wisp of pleasure. Is it any wonder why coughing, congestion,
asthma, and an ever-increasing number of respiratory problems
appear? When our respiratory system gives us problems, we
assault it with more chemical inhalants, artificial cough suppres-
sants, and synthetic anti-histamines. By this time, not only do the
pollutants work against the normal body function, but the "medicine" further violates the body's principles.

The body deliberately breathes shallowly to take in as little
pollution as possible. The lungs try to expel the mucus which they
must form to protect themselves from the irritation. Instead of
joining forces with the body, the "medication" invades and attempts to take care of the problem in its own way.

How much better it would be if the afflicted person would learn
proper breathing, get adequate exercise, and supplement the diet
with vitamins and herbs which cleanse, equip and fortify the
body's respiratory functions (see Chapter 11, Herbal Combinations).

The Second Principle:
Proper Food, the Basis for Good Health

Soon after our little Abner takes his first breath, he will
instinctively set about to meet his second basic need, finding food.
He seems to intuitively realize that his future growth and health
depend on his food supply. While he may not be very discriminat-
ing, and might settle for a prepared formula or the milk from a
bovine creature, if we observe carefully, we will note that he is not
saying "moo" nor was he made in a factory!

The first step in cooperating with this natural need for food is
to feed this new human body human mother's milk. Provided the
mother is healthy, her milk is the best and most specifically
formulated food supply for that baby. In addition to the proper
equation of nutrients, it also contains digestive enzymes, intestinal flora and immunity factors. All of these are so important and
basic for a proper start toward good health. In some developing
countries where "baby formula marketeers" have been able to
persuade mothers to use formula milk instead of their own, the
health of babies has suffered dramatically. An indication of how
unnatural and commercialized our society has become is a young

mother who recently remarked," Oh yes, I know that nursing is the newest thing out, but I'll stay with the old way of bottle feeding."

Parents, if you want to raise a calf, logically you would feed it cow's milk. If you want to raise a junk food addict, logically you would feed it formula and sugar-spiked baby foods. Baby food manufacturers have confessed that the main reason they need to add so much sugar to the baby food is to satisfy the taste of the mother. Mother, the best way to start your child toward a healthy life is to feed her with beautiful, love-enriched breast milk, and do it for as long as possible — at least six months. Parents care so much about when their baby will take that first step; helping that child in these first steps toward good health is even more important.

At this point I could well go into great detail on good eating. Eat natural, organic, raw, non-processed, grease-free foods, avoiding additives, flavorings, colorings, and so forth. Since this could fill a book in itself, I would simply stress: eat food that is natural and works with your body rather than against it.

Next to air and food, and perhaps even more important then food, is water. It seems that while our society has become obsessed with outward cleanliness, and while water is used in abundance for this purpose, inner cleanliness and the amount of water we drink has decreased. Keep in mind that water is the universal solvent. It cleanses not only on the outside, but also on the inside. Many people who do not drink enough water are chronically dehydrated. The body tissues and fluids become thicker and more viscid. The kidneys find it impossible to thoroughly cleanse and remove the impurities from the blood, and the general toxicity level in the body increases.

I believe that an unconscious reason that many do not drink enough water is because of a distaste for all the impurities in the water. It has become almost impossible to have pure water without water purification. For adequate and effective water treatment, I have had to conclude that the most effective way to purify water is by reverse osmosis or distillation. Do not worry about losing the minerals. Drinking water is not a significant source of mineral intake. Besides, the minerals in the water are inorganic and probably do more harm than good. Provide pure, clean water for yourself and drink it freely. Doing this alone has improved the health of many people.

The Third Principle: Elimination

If we return again for a moment to our little Abner, we will notice that another normal function, elimination, is also an un-avoidable part of natural good health. While this is not an enjoyable topic, its neglect and abuse lies at the root of many health problems. Since this matter involves the entire Chapter 4, I would simply remind the reader here that unless you get and stay in step with your body's elimination functions, good health cannot be assured. Learn and practice ways to help your body rid itself of toxicity and waste material in a complete and regular way.

The Fourth Principle:
Immune Function for Top Defense

Our little Abner is fortunately equipped with an amazing defense system. This system is prepared to defend his body from bacteria, virus and disease. To work with this system, and to join forces with it is the wisest step one can take toward good health. Unwittingly, many find themselves working against this wonderful defense system rather than with it. It has become almost standard procedure for the new parents to feel obligated to take little Abner to the doctor if he coughs or sneezes more than once. The doctor is also obligated to give the baby antibiotics and thus unknowingly denies the body the opportunity to gain experience in building up its own natural defensive capacity. No wonder little Abner easily becomes dependent on medication! This area is so significant we have taken Chapter 5 to deal with it.

According to reason and experience, we are assured that if little Abner will learn and follow the secrets of cooperating with his body, health and longevity will be his. We also believe that if his Aunt Mary and Uncle John who have already developed health complications will follow the advice given here and in the following chapters, they also can regain their natural good health.

19

Chapter 3

Nutrition,
the First Step
in Human Health

Today, rampant health breakdown is upon us. We are experiencing a harvest of disease, the fruit of a "chemicalized" environment and a toxic internal condition. Yet, the popular alternative responses only seem to speed the breakdown. The time has come to take the first step toward natural good health.

In this chapter you will discover:

• What is the basic factor of human existence, what it does, and what it needs.

• How our chemical environment frustrates this factor.

• Why "eating right" and taking a "one-a-day" pill is not enough.

• How you can join forces with your body to activate its normal function.

Increased Energy

My wife and I have been following Dr. Zehr's Maintenance Programs. We both have noticed a definite increase in energy and a general feeling of increased well-being.

R.R.

When I got home from work I used to always need at least one hour of rest before I could start dinner for my family. After being on Dr. Zehr's Maintenance Program, I no longer need that rest. I have lots of energy!

S.A.

An Absolute Asset

I'm one of those fortunate people who has always enjoyed good health. But as an active woman and mother, I have found Dr. Zehr's Maintenance Program to be an absolute asset to me.

C.N.

When we consider the matter of human health and well-being, we must begin our consideration with the first and most basic principle of human existence, life. This may seem obvious yet it is often overlooked. The central and most crucial factor of human existence is life. Our very essence and sense of being is a matter of life. Of course there is life on several levels: physical, psychological, and spiritual, but here we will concern ourselves with how to preserve and maintain the human physical life in order for it to realize and experience its fullest potential.

The Life Factor

Since life is the beginning factor, with it rests the basic principles of our well-being and existence. If we accept and harmonize with these basic principles, life will accomplish its desires. As we have pointed out in the first two chapters, this means that the body will maintain wellness and even bring itself back to wellness if it is not well. So, let us consider a few of these basic principles.

Life is Natural

Life is natural and organic. Unless we were made in a test tube or fathered by a robot, then every cell of our body is a living

23

organic element. Anything that is synthetic, inorganic, or artificial is alien and foreign to the body. While it may enter and even affect the body, it cannot fully harmonize with the body because it is of a different nature. This principle should show us clearly that although drugs, chemicals and even synthetic supplements may affect the body, their ability to join forces with the body and to assist it in its way of healing is very limited.

Life is Self-Rejuvenating

A further amazing characteristic of life is that it is self-rejuvenating and self-healing. Of all the inventions of man, none can heal and restore itself. Yet, an exhausted, weak and worn-down body can, with rest and nourishment, renew and strengthen itself provided there are life elements available in the food supply. Furthermore, the life element in the body can heal an open wound or mend a broken bone easily if its healing forces are adequately supplied. Recent experiments have shown that this same life force can even rebuild a partial liver to wholeness.

Life Depends on Supply

All this amazing life capacity is available to the human body provided that its needs are met in these three areas: it must receive proper nutrition; it must experience adequate cleansing and elimination; and its innate defense, that is the immune system, must be functioning effectively. At the same time, we must be conscious of the fact that a violation or non-compliance with these life factors frustrates and breaks down the physical body. If the breakdown exceeds the rebuilding, health deteriorates and sickness becomes inevitable. Our interest in this chapter is to consider the case for nutrition in order to adequately meet the need for physical life to realize its potential.

The Decline of Nutrition

Our Natural Past

In mankind's early history, food was primarily fresh, eaten raw, and mostly in season. The capacity to process or refine was very limited. Additives and preservatives, other than natural elements were unheard of. If land did not produce, compost or manure was applied, or the field was allowed to "rest" until nature could restore its natural elements. All this meant that the "life" elements in the food were naturally present and available to meet the life needs of the body. Most of the sickness and disease surrounding us today were virtually unheard of under such conditions.

Our Chemical Present

Today, our soil is overworked and constantly "chemicalized." Insects are destroyed by chemical insecticides and weeds are killed by chemical herbicides. After the food products (which are already low in nutritional value) are harvested, they are processed, flavored, cooked, baked, barbecued and then "over-eaten." By this time, the life elements which the human body depends on are so limited that it becomes almost impossible for the body to maintain normal good health. Take a live green tomato and with time it will ripen by the innate life force. Cook the same tomato and in a short time it will rot. This shows how the life element is lost even in cooking. Add to this the increased stress of pollution and complex lifestyle; the stage is set for rampant health breakdown. Consider the following facts.

The Disease Harvest

Presently over one million people per year (that is 3,000 per day) die of heart disease in North America. This disease was almost unheard of in primitive society. An increasing number of people suffer from mental illness. Although Dr. Abram Hoffer showed years ago that many could be helped with B Vitamin supplementation, very few psychiatrists today realize that a dietary deficiency may also underlie mental illness.

There are approximately forty million arthritis sufferers in the United States with an increase of over one million annually. The millions of diabetic and osteoporosis sufferers are increasing daily. Diabetes is very clearly related to diet. At the same time, statistics show that seventy-five per cent of women consume less than two-thirds of the calcium suggested by the United States Recommended Daily Allowances (USRDA).

Our Chemical Response

Meanwhile, it seems that our health care establishment, instead of supplying our innate life power with natural organic and life-complementary forces, has turned almost entirely to chemical, invasive and drug therapies. Besides violating the basic life factors, much of the present approach adds further stress and frustration. Eventually, one-third of all hospital patients are hospitalized as a result of medical complications rather than from simple physical illness.

Alternative Responses

Hang in There

Now let us conscientiously consider the alternatives before us. The most common one, seldom chosen, but often ours by default, is to simply "hang in there" and hope that our body will not break down. If and when it does break down, we will do what we can to restore it. The sad fact is that health breakdown is occurring at an increasingly earlier age than in the past. The problems that began to afflict my parents at sixty seem to have come to my generation in their forties, and are already appearing in my children's generation in their twenties. It seems that very few children do not have allergies, and we find that even diabetes and arthritis are now found among them.

Turn Back the Clock

Some concerned persons have concluded that the best option is to try to turn back the clock. Return to a primitive diet and lifestyle. Eat only organic and seasonal foods, avoid air and water pollution, and get away from the stress and fatigue of the "jet-age" pace. To whatever extent one can do this in a realistic and practical way it, certainly has merit, but for most of us such a course of action seems quite impossible.

Technical Diagnosis

If the resources and expertise are available, one may choose to get a detailed diagnosis of the body's nutrient status and then try to take specific supplementary elements to meet the need. This may be the ideal response if deficiencies are evident. For

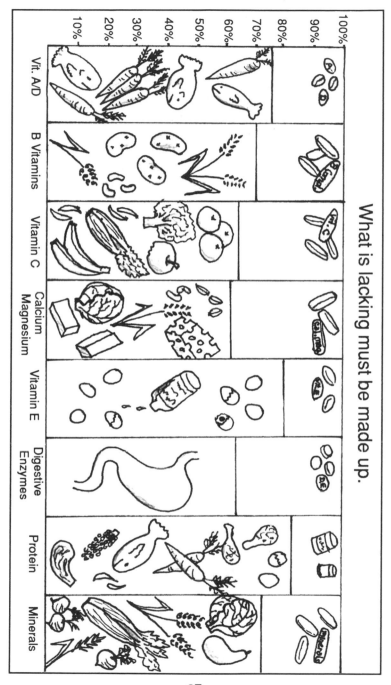

What is lacking must be made up.

normal situations and for the average person, however, this method may be both difficult and impractical.

Comprehensive Supplement Assurance

Surely the above backdrop establishes a strong case for supplementation. But let us be clear what we mean when we refer to supplementation, and that our definition is according to "life" principles. By supplementation we mean an additional supply of the essential elements that the body utilizes to maintain health vitality. The purpose for supplementation is to join forces with the body to activate the body's normal functions according to life principles.

From this, one might conclude that an economical, synthetic "one-a-day" might be the easy way to go. But rather, such a product should be considered a marketeer's exploitation of a need. It is the offering of a cheap substitute for the real thing. Since this appeals to the "take a pill" mentality, it seems logical. Be aware, however, that life is not synthetic, and synthetic is not life. Because this has been accepted as the answer to the dilemma, but has not proven effective, many people or consumers are closed to the real answer.

Based upon the present situation and the alternatives available, I would suggest, as the most realistic solution, a broad-based comprehensive natural nutritional supplement program. Such a program should incorporate the following principles: it must use natural, organic source nutrients as much as possible; it must be comprehensive enough to cover all the areas of possible need; it should consider timing for maximum body efficiency. (This accounts for the fact that some nutrients may be more effective in the morning and others in the evening.)

The ideal program must also consider synergistic factors, realizing that some elements complement each other such as vitamin E and selenium. Others are antagonistic, meaning that they may compete for binding sites and are best not taken simultaneously. Biochemically, males and females have unique needs, and this should be accounted for in an ideal program. I prefer to add a digestive enzyme compound to assure maximum digestion and assimilation. Finally, since nutrients are naturally found in plants and are often activated by herbs, it is preferable that they be blended in an herbal base.

The following suggestions are given as an example of a program that incorporates the above ideals. I believe this to be the most realistic response to the desperate need to reinforce the crucial life factors which maintain health in the midst of the complexities of modern civilization.

A Model Program

In the morning for men and women:
1 Multi Vitamin Mineral †
Calcium 300 mg with Magnesium 150 mg
Selenium 100 mcg
Vitamin E (d-Alpha tocopherol with mixed tocopherols)
Calcium Pangamate

With the evening meal:

for women:
1 Multi Vitamin Mineral †
Vitamin C 500 mg
Calcium 300 mg with Magnesium 150 mg
Iron 35 mg
Digestive Enzyme Supplement †
Female Multi Glandular †

for men:
1 Multi Vitamin Mineral †
Vitamin C 500 mg
Zinc 25 mg
Digestive Enzyme Supplement †
Male Multi Glandular †

Chapter 4

Cleansing — an Indispensable Step for Keeping Well

Rest, exercise, good food and supplements should be rewarded with health, vigor and lots of energy. If this is not the case, there must be a thief, stealing, pilfering or just slowly draining the life supply. Perhaps it is time to look deeper, even to the depths of our being, to find the answer.

In this chapter you will discover:

• Why cleansing is so important, what it does, and why your body needs it.

• Why colon health is so essential for overall body health.

• Why you may be suffering from a congested colon and how to recognize some telltale symptoms.

• How you can become "squeaky clean" from the inside out.

Besides adequate nutritional intake, the human body requires elimination. Stale, "used" air is exhaled through breathing. The sweat glands and kidneys work to eliminate polluted "used" water and the bowels work to process and pass bacteria and unuseable food stuff. These elimination activities may also be refered to as cleansing or detoxification.

While people assume that these processes are normal and need no special attention, the following reports and the information in this chapter will show how supporting the body's cleansing and detoxification activities has become almost indispensable in today's environment.

A Must at Least Twice a Year

Most people come to me with lazy bowels or toxins. After Dr. Zehr's Body Cleansing and Detoxification Program, they feel terrific. This program should be done at least twice a year to keep feeling good.

B.A.

Brings Relief from Asthma

Dr. Zehr's Body Cleansing and Detoxification Program is a wonderful two week program which not only cleanses the body but seems to cleanse the cobwebs in the head too. My son with asthma found this program to cleanse all his mucus, giving him a fresh start. I have just finished following Dr. Zehr's program for the sixth time.

W.D.

From Acne to Glowing Face in Four Weeks

I had tried everything from dermatologists to Chinese herbs and facials. Nothing would work and I couldn't find out what was causing my facial acne. It completely covered my face with large extremely sore pimples that even hurt in the shower.

At 28, I had teenage acne all over again, or so I thought.Then after about a year, I met a wonderful woman who suggested Dr. Zehr's Body Cleansing and Detoxification and Yeast Control Programs. Within four weeks, I was so happy! I felt great! My body

33

was clean and my face was glowing! I felt like a new person! Today, my skin is a mirror of how my body is feeling — fantastic!"
K.M.

A Cure for My Bowel Problems

For many years I went to many doctors trying to find a cure for my bowel problems, digestive problems and the discomfort I could not seem to escape from. Finally the doctors would just look at me with sad eyes that seemed to say, "You poor lady, you need a head doctor." Then I found out about Dr. Zehr's Body Cleansing and Detoxification Program. What a relief!
L.S.

The great concern of the Ninety's has to be the environment. The problem with the environment is pollution. Unless we do two things, clean up the environment and stop polluting it, we will commit a slow suicide for ourselves and a fast suicide for our children. Our world is becoming sick. Wildlife, plants, trees, forests and even the ozone layer, all are dying. Unless action is taken, our planet earth will be sick — unto death.

An equally great and urgent concern for all of us must be what I hereby name the "invironment." While the environment is the atmosphere and surroundings in which we live, the "invironment" is the atmosphere and surroundings inside of us. The same problem that is plaguing the environment is also plaguing the invironment. Pollution is as threatening and damaging inside of us as it is outside of us.

Here also, unless we do two things, stop polluting and clean up the existing pollution, we will become more and more plagued with sickness and will commit a slow suicide. Already this is the experience of many people.

Today, most of our ill health is due to the pollution in our invironment. This chapter is concerned about cleaning up that pollution. The information presented has brought healing and cleansing to thousands of polluted invironments, and I trust will help you as well.

Next time someone tells you about their concern for the environment, ask them if they have considered the condition of their own *invironment*.

In recent years a growing number of health authorities are concluding that poor bowel function and colon blockage are key factors behind most of mankind's illnesses.

Three of these well-known professionals strike a sobering note: V.E. Irons, a noted bowel specialist says, "In my opinion, there is only one real disease, and that disease is autointoxication — the body poisoning itself. It's the filth in our system that kills us. So, I'm convinced that unless you clean out your colon you will never regain vibrant health."

Dr. Bernard Jensen summarizes his findings, "In the fifty years I've spent helping people to overcome disability and disease, it has become crystal clear that poor bowel management lies at the root of most people's health problems. In treating over 300,000 patients, it is the bowel that invariably has to be cared for first before effective healing can take place."

Dr. Norman Walker explains, "Good health not only regenerates and rebuilds the cells and tissues which constitute your physical body, but also is involved in the processes by which the waste matter, the undigested food, is eliminated from your body to prevent corruption in the form of fermentation and putrefaction. This corruption, if retained and allowed to accumulate in the body, prevents any possibility of attaining any degree of vibrant health. …Not to cleanse the colon," Dr. Walker concludes, "is like having the entire garbage collection staff in your city go on strike for days on end. The accumulation of garbage in the streets creates putrid, odoriferous, unhealthy gases which are dispersed into the atmosphere."

The Colon — Its Parts and Function

The colon, also known as the large intestine and bowel, is probably one of the least appreciated organs of the body, yet a basic understanding of its function is absolutely necessary for anyone seeking to achieve and maintain good heath. The colon is a large muscular organ about five feet (1.5 m) long which lies at the end of the digestive tract. (See Figure 1.)

Digested food (chyme) is received into the cecum, the lower part of the ascending colon, through the ileo cecal valve. At the lowest extremity of the cecum, even lower than the ileo cecal

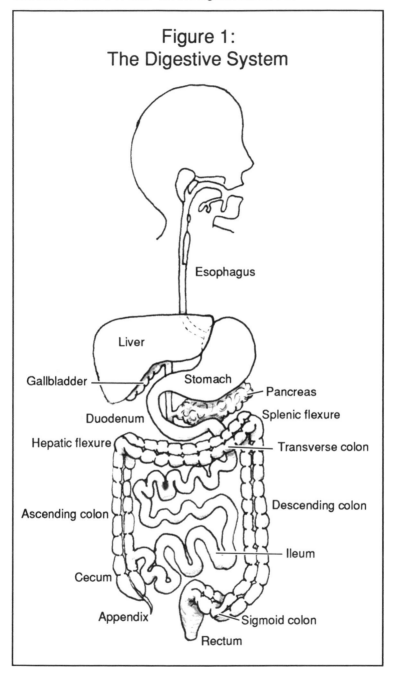

Figure 1:
The Digestive System

Esophagus

Liver

Gallbladder

Stomach

Pancreas

Duodenum

Splenic flexure

Hepatic flexure

Transverse colon

Ascending colon

Descending colon

Ileum

Cecum

Appendix

Sigmoid colon

Rectum

valve, is a small fingerlike appendage called the appendix. For years, the appendix has been labeled a useless organ, but recent research indicates that it may play an important role in proper colon function. In fact, some colon experts have collected data showing that appendicitis occurs when the colon is not functioning properly. If the appendix is removed, more colon problems are often the result.

If colon function is sluggish, the lowest part of the cecum is also a favorite lodging place of parasites. The parasites will feast on the nutrients in the chyme and will enjoy undisturbed repose so long as the bowel remains in its sluggish state.

The chyme received into the cecum is semi-liquid and consists of undigested or indigestible food substances, water, and secretions from the liver, pancreas and small intestine. In the cecum area much of the water is withdrawn and absorbed.

Bacterial action now begins to play a major role in the completion of the digestion process. Billions of friendly bacteria synthesize valuable nutrients by digesting some of the fecal mass. Vitamin K, and some of the B vitamins, as well as other nutrients are produced. Some remaining proteins are broken down into simpler substances. No digestive enzymes are secreted in the colon, but an alkaline fluid aids in the completion of digestion begun in the small intestines.

During this process the chyme is pushed up the ascending colon, around the hepatic flexure and across the transverse colon toward the splenic flexure. (See Figure 1.) This movement is the result of peristaltic action which is caused by the muscles in the bulbous pouches of the colon walls. As the chyme moves, positive bacteria and more moisture are withdrawn.

As the material enters the descending colon, it is called feces. Toxic waste from the blood system is received and

Figure 2: The Normal Colon

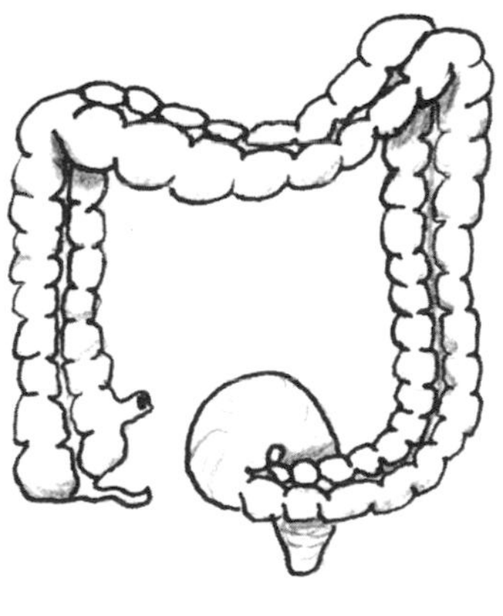

carried with the fecal material toward the sigmoid colon and then the rectum. By this time, feces contain putrefying bacteria and waste products

The amount of time, "transit time," for this process depends on the amount of roughage in the food, the water content, and the condition of the colon.

When the fecal material arrives in the lower descending colon it should be formed in large soft stools and should be evacuated in a consistent and effortless way. Since by this time it contains putrefactive elements and toxic waste, it must be discharged regularly and completely or ill health will result.

Colon Complications Steal Health and Vigor

If the food eaten is not fresh, unprocessed, vital and full of the roughage of raw foods, it is difficult for the body to move it through the digestive tract. Over time it will leave layer after layer of slime, like plaster on a wall, on the inner walls of the colon. Oily, greasy and mucus-forming foods, like dairy products, will add to this encrustation. As a child, I watched people make wallpaper paste from white flour and water. Yet, today still millions of people eat that same paste, plastering their colons with layer after layer of this gooey, sticky coating.

Eventually, this "plaster" may accumulate to the point where there is only a small hole in the center of the colon through which chyme and feces must pass. Yet, it is through that thick accumulation that the body must try to pull nutrients. It is little wonder that so many people, though they try to eat well and may even take supplements, just do not feel as good as they should. Most of the good food and supplements are going right through them! Dr. Walker declares, "The consequent result is a starvation of which we are not conscious, but which causes old age and senility to race toward us with the throttle wide open." (See Figure 3.)

If chyme and feces in the colon are not moved along and eliminated from the body regularly, they will begin to ferment and putrefy much like waste in a sewage system would if it were allowed to back up.

When we realize that the colon is the sanitation department of our body, we may tend to want to forget that it exists. However, a city would soon be plagued with ill health, disease and parasitic

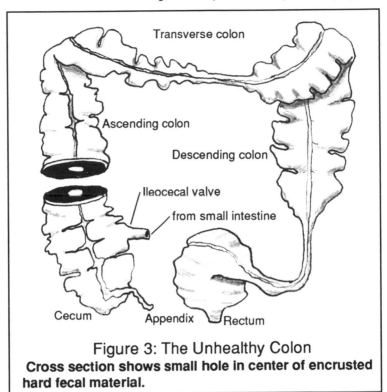

Figure 3: The Unhealthy Colon
Cross section shows small hole in center of encrusted hard fecal material.

infestation if it neglected its sanitation system. Yet, very few people consider that their constant state of fatigue, sickness, and lethargy may be the result of a neglected sanitation system.

When a person eats well, takes supplements and gets some exercise but still feels dragged out and "blah", chances are he may be suffering from autointoxication. Dr. Bernard Jensen describes autointoxication as "the result of faulty bowel functioning which produces undesirable consequences in the body and is the root cause of many of today's diseases and illnesses." The rotting fecal material produces toxicity and poison which, because of the congested colon, the body cannot rid itself of. Therefore, what little nutritional element the body can absorb is polluted! The body is toxifying itself! This toxicity is carried by the blood throughout the body and a host of health problems may result.

Since the colon has relatively few nerve endings, it can

withstand considerable abuse without registering significant pain. Consequently, many abnormalities may develop before one is aware of a problem.

Diverticulitis is the result of an undue amount of pressure

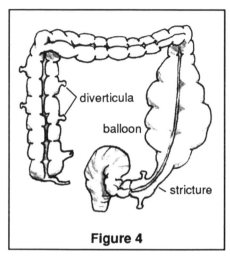

diverticula

balloon

stricture

Figure 4

occurring when the colon tries to squeeze the hard feces in order to keep them moving. This tends to cause a hernia, producing a small pouch-like sack in the tissue. After feces accumulate they become morbid and may become inflamed. (See Figure 4.)

Colitis is a somewhat general term that refers to inflammation of the colon. This inflammation usually begins with a rupture or from the decomposition of accummulated blocked fecal material.

Spastic Bowel is the result of the colon muscle being overworked, tense, and not adequately rested. This is a chronic tightening of the fibers of the muscles.

Ballooning is the result of backed up feces. The feces can accumulate and stretch the bowel walls to enormous proportions.

Stricture is a chronic narrowing of the colon passageway usually resulting from inflammation. The feces accumulating in front of the stricture may develop ballooning so that the segment just past the stricture may collapse and the muscles become atrophied or inoperative (see figure 4).

Prolapsus is when the transverse colon falls or collapses probably due to an overload of accumulated

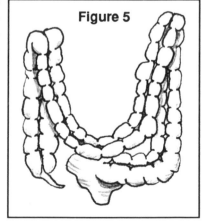

Figure 5

waste (see figure 5). The fallen part may begin to rest on the lower organs and may become a problem especially for females. The abnormal pressure needed to force the feces through the hepatic and splenic flexure may also become a problem.

Who is Affected

While we might expect this to be the problem of some careless few, Dr. Harvey W. Kellog, M.D. says, "Of the 22,000 operations I personally performed, I never found a single normal colon and of the 100,000 performed under my jurisdiction not over six per cent were normal."

Dr. Norman Walker, a specialist in colon health, states, "If a person has eaten processed, fried and overcooked foods, devitalized starches, sugar and excessive amounts of salt, his colon cannot possibly be efficient, even if he should have a bowel movement two to three times a day!"

Recently a man in his mid-thirties came to me with the x-rays of his colon. Although it was grossly misshapen and did not empty itself properly, the pathologist reported that its condition was "normal."

I would feel that everyone seeking to attain or maintain better health should be concerned about the condition of his colon. Over the years, in the course of helping thousands of people on the pathway to better health, I have observed that colon congestion is one of the most fundamental problems. Pimples, acne, and other skin problems are often simply the body's attempt to rid itself of what the colon cannot.

A Colon Management Program

A sober look at the situation makes it clear that the need for proper bowel management and colon cleansing is acute. Much research and experimentation has been done, especially by the aforementioned experts. After having carefully studied their findings and conducted further experiments, I am happy to present a specific program. The basic factors in this program are bentonite and psyllium seeds and husks.

When the accumulated debris in the colon has been removed, the invironment has been cleaned up. Then the body's resources are fully available to supply the demands of an active life and the solution to pollution has begun!

After studying and experimenting with the programs suggested by various experts, I have brought together the strengths of each and put forward a program as follows:

The 14 Day way to:
Health Restoration through Colon Evacuation

This program is designed to generate a progressive cleansing effect on the body. It does this in three phases. These phases are in complete harmony with normal body function so that there is very little interference with normal routine or daily activity. If the colon is congested and bowel function is poor, I suggest you repeat it once every two months. Otherwise, twice yearly should maintain adequate bowel function.

It may be hard to comprehend that so much is taking place in one's body, but after the program has been completed one should realize a new sense of vigor and well-being.

Phase 1 — Preparation (7 Days)
This phase prepares the colon for cleansing while it draws the toxic buildup from the entire system and brings it to the colon. The herbal intestinal cleanse formula loosens the mucus on the walls of the small intestine. The herbal detoxification formula will stimulate the body to release latent toxicity being held in the glands and tissues. Unless a person exercises and sweats regularly, he probably is "holding" a great amount of toxic waste. The other supplements bring the body into a good nutritional state and also bring the colon and bowels into proper function. If stools become too loose, take only one Cascara Sagrada per day.

Take morning and evening:
       1 Multi vitamin mineral †
       Vitamin C 500 mg.
       Acidophilus (1 billion)
       Cascara sagrada tablet (450 mg)
       Alfalfa tablets (1000 mg)
       2 Herbal detoxification formula †
       2 Herbal intestinal cleanse formula †

The <u>multi</u> should be an all-natural mega vitamin/mineral to assure nutritional balance throughout the entire program.

<u>Vitamin C</u> is an anti-oxidant and infection fighter and is important to maintain resistance to the toxic activity generated by the cleansing process.

<u>Acidophilus</u> helps to maintain a positive bacteria environment in the intestine.

<u>Cascara Sagrada</u> acts as a natural laxative, softening the stools and lubricating the bowels with a soothing, healing oil.

<u>Alfalfa</u> provides a broad base of minerals and is also a source of chlorophyl, sometimes referred to as stored sunshine.

<u>Herbal Detoxification Formula</u> is a combination of herbs consisting of Garlic, Chaparral, Foenugreek, Quassia, Red Sage, Black Cohosh, and Golden Seal. Traditional use of these herbs has been for general cleansing of the body.

<u>Herbal Intestinal Cleanse Formula</u> is an herbal combination containing Comfrey, Pepsin and Wheat Germ. This formula, an herbal and digestive combination, was popularized by Dr. William D. Kelley, who uses it to dissolve the mucous film which coats the small intestine of many individuals.

Phase 2 — Cleansing (4 Days)

During this phase we are softening the accumulated encrusted fecal material from the walls of the colon. In one case, a person had not eaten grapes for years; grape seeds were passed. Often great quantities of fecal material will be discharged. Strong odors may be present as the accumulated toxicity of phase one is eliminated from the body.

Take morning and evening:
    1 Multi vitamin mineral †
    Vitamin C 500 mg.
    Acidophilus (1 billion)
    Cascara sagrada tablet (450 mg)
    Alfalfa tablets (1000 mg)
    1 Herbal detoxification formula †
    1 Herbal intestinal cleanse formula †

In addition take five times daily or every three hours:one heaping teaspoon psyllium husks and 1.5 tablespoons hydrated bentonite in an eight ounce glass of unsweetened fruit or vegetable juice; shake well and drink immediately; follow with one glass of water. Do not mix these ingredients beforehand because they will gel within minutes. If you need to take them to work, keep them in separate containers.

Take no solid foods and no other liquids except unsweetened juices, mild herbal teas, and water. The powder will swell up in your system and you should not feel hungry. Take *at least* one glass of water during intervals between dosages. If regularity is a problem, an enema of tepid water (body temperature) each night might be helpful.

Hydrated Bentonite is made from volcanic ash. It acts like a magnetic sponge to remove toxins from the digestive tract. In fact, this amazing substance absorbs up to forty times its own weight in toxic substances! This keeps the toxins from being reabsorbed into the system as they are passing out of the colon. It also loosens stagnant material and lifts hardened mucoid off the colon wall. Psyllium husk removes the material that the bentonite has loosened. It swells enormously with water, forming a bulky, jelly-like medium that has the amazing ability to absorb large quantities of sticky, gluey mucoid and still maintain its slippery, non-sticky lubricating nature. The resulting redissolved waste can be passed easily from the body.

By the middle of this phase you should begin to see dramatic results. Check your stools for information and encouragement. Don't be shy. Your inside story is your business, and the information it yields may be of great help to your future health.

If due to sugar imbalance or for other reasons, food must be eaten, simply eat as needed. The overall value may be less, but the experience will still be very worthwhile.

If the effect during phase one or phase two seems to be too severe, then reduce the dosage to half the amount or to whatever rate the body is able to accomodate. If the dosage is decreased, simply extend the overall length of time. This gives the body the same total cleansing but over a longer time period.

Phase 3 — Restoration (3 Days)
Take morning and evening:
1 Multi vitamin mineral †
Vitamin C 500 mg.
2 Acidophilus (1 billion)
Cascara sagrada tablet (400 mg)
Alfalfa tablets (1000 mg)
1 Digestive Enzyme Supplement †

The additional acidophilus is intended to help restore the intestinal flora which may be somewhat reduced by the intense cleansing in Phase 2.

The digestive enzyme supplement should contain Papain, Pepsin, Bile Salts, Pancreatin, and Betaine Hydrochloride to assure good digestion following the Phase 2 juice diet.

To give the digestive system a chance to gradually resume its normal workload, eat only raw and lightly cooked vegetables on the first day. You may begin to eat small portions of protein, such as eggs and meats, on the second day of this phase. Do not try to make up for lost time by gorging yourself. You will probably find that your body needs and has room for less food than before. When your body says, "full," stop eating, even if your mind says, "you should be eating more." Psyllium husks and bentonite may be taken twice daily until movements become regular and normal.

The program I've described will take you through a major step in cleaning up the pollution in your inner invironment. The next step, to stop polluting, must follow. By following the steps outlined in this book as well as in the suggested readings in Appendix D, significant steps can be taken to keep your invironment clean and thereby assure yourself the good health that is naturally yours.

Chapter 5

Getting in Step with the Body's Defensive Army

Every human body has an amazing capacity to preserve and protect itself. If this capacity is lost, there are millions of attackers ready and available to invade and to work havoc in the human system.

In the coming years, all who wish to survive and enjoy health and vitality *must* learn to know and care about the body's own health-keeper — the IMMUNE SYSTEM.

In this chapter you will discover:

• Why you could not survive a day without your immune system.

• Why some medications may actually undermine your body's natural ability to fight against sickness.

• How your body fights cancer, AIDS and other diseases.

• How you can cooperate with your immune system to protect yourself from disease.

The human body's amazing capacity to protect itself against disease has long been recognized and respected, yet taken for granted. Recent health breakdown coupled with tireless workers in the preventive medicine field have opened a whole new era of interest in the immune system.

Brings More Energy and Enthusiasm

Before I started on Dr. Zehr's Immune Support Program, I felt very run down with low energy. I could not get enthusiastic about anything. I had to have coffee in the afternoon and had to go to bed at 10:30 PM; I would fall asleep immediately. After even 10 or 11 hours of sleep, I would still not feel rested. About 10 days after starting the Program, I realized that I no longer needed the coffee and I was staying up until midnight and then forcing myself to go to bed. I was waking up without an alarm clock, full of enthusiasm.

K.K.

Relief from Hayfever

After suffering from hayfever for years and not wanting to use antihistamines, I was delighted after just one day on Dr. Zehr's Immune Support Program to discover that I had very few hayfever symptoms. After being on the Program for one week, I had absolutely no hayfever.

B.G.

No More Allergy Symptoms

My husband and I have had allergies for about four years: sneezing, runny eyes, itchy eyes and ears, and so on. These symptoms would last over four months every year. This year when we started to have our allergies in May, we started on Dr. Zehr's Immune Support Program. After one month, our allergies have disappeared.

G.K.

No More Environmental Sensitivities

A teenager came to me after being hospitalized by sensitivities to common environmental substances and foods. He was forced to abstain from sports and physical activities. He followed Dr. Zehr's Immune Support Program for three months and then went on the Maintenance Program [see Chapter 3]. His allergies cleared up rapidly. He was able to resume an active life which included a French immersion program in France over the summer.

C.F.

Let us consider the body as a massive collection of 60 trillion cells contained within a semi-permeable membrane called skin. These cells are varied in their make-up and arranged so as to form different organs and systems. These organs and systems are appropriately assembled to form the human body, and work together to allow this body to operate and perform its normal functions.

It is these cells which form the very basis of the human body and they have much in common. They recognize and accept each other, are all organic and resist anything foreign or inorganic. Each cell contains within itself the mechanism to replicate, that is to replace itself, which it does periodically as long as its host is alive. Within each cell is a blueprint containing details not only of its own makeup, but of that of the entire body. It is because of this blueprint that the cells in a body can recognize, accept and harmonize with all other cells within that same body. However, because of that same blueprint, they will refuse to accept any entity which is not from or of themselves.

The body, made up of these cells, exists in a very hostile environment. It is surrounded by many enemies some of which find ways to enter the body and there harass and disturb it. Some of these enemies, such as yeast and fungi, attempt to reproduce, colonize, and then decompose the body. Others such as viruses try to afflict the body with sickness and disease. Still others like bacteria are determined to spread putrefaction and death.

Then there is the dreaded disease, cancer, which occurs when the cell's ability to reproduce itself goes out of control. Today, we face the most sinister and vicious enemy of all, AIDS. AIDS works to re-tool the cell's own machinery to make it become a factory to produce more AIDS virus. (More about this later.)

With such an array of enemies it becomes obvious that for the cells to survive, and even more for them to function in a healthy way, it is very necessary for there to be a strong and active defense system. The body needs a system that will protect the cells, identify the enemies, and then destroy them. The fact that we are alive is proof that there is such a system. This system is the IMMUNE SYSTEM.

The Immune System — How it Works

Why do some people catch everything that comes along while others do not? Why do children tend to get chicken pox, measles, mumps, and other childhood diseases only once? Why

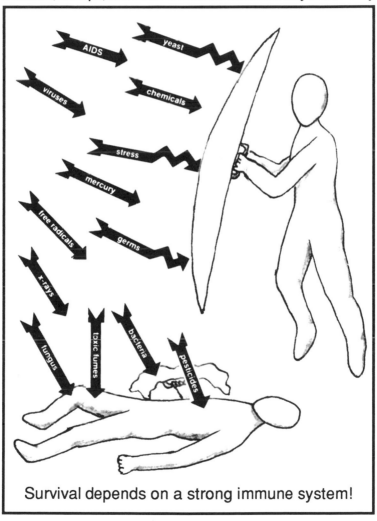

Survival depends on a strong immune system!

are children and chronically ill older persons more susceptible to flu and viral diseases? Why is it so difficult for the human body to accept an organ transplant? The answers to these and many more such questions lie in a basic understanding of the body's immune system.

Having noted that the cells are the basic component of the human body, it is evident that they must be cared for, nourished and maintained in a proper biochemical environment. In addition, the cells must also be protected from the constant barrage of attacks from their numerous enemies. Today's environment and lifestyle put our bodies at a distinct disadvantage. Pollution in air, water and food frustrates and damages cellular function and collaborates with the enemies by weakening the body. Constant interaction with people from around the world exposes us to large numbers of viruses, fungi and bacteria. One hour at a busy international airport can expose one to as many "global germs" as our greatgrandparents probably confronted in a lifetime.

Immune Response

The immune system's first response to an enemy attack might be referred to as detection and rejection. The detection mechanism is very precise. When anything foreign to the body is discovered, an alarm sounds which alerts and activates the rejection forces.

This is why organ transplants were considered to be such a medical breakthrough. When an organ transplant is attempted, the host's immune forces immediately detect and identify as "alien" the cells of this new organ. Anything alien or foreign is to be rejected. In an attempt to avoid this rejection, medical doctors try to transplant the organ of a near relative whom they hope has a cellular blueprint similar enough to fool the immune system. Since the immune system cannot be fooled, drugs are usually administered to weaken the immune response so that it is unable to reject the new organ. This, of course, makes the host dangerously susceptible to infection and disease. From this we see how sensitive and particular the immune system is.

Viruses Beware!

To further understand the immune system's players and their respective activities, assume that a flu virus has invaded the body.

It may have entered through air you breathed, through a cut or through something you touched. However it entered, its intention is to find lodging in the tissues and feed off the body's nutrients so that it can thrive and multiply. Its goal is to take over the cells, disrupting their normal function and using them for its own purposes. As soon as this virus enters the bloodstream, it begins to multiply, and if left unchecked will eventually destroy the body's function. The progress of this unsuspecting invader, however, does not go unnoticed.

Lymphocytes and T-cells

A certain kind of white blood cell known as lymphocytes constantly patrol both the circulatory system and the area of fluid immediately surrounding the cells. Some of these lymphocytes pass through the thymus gland, a small walnut-sized organ at the base of the neck where they receive some special hormone treatment and become T-cells. (T, of course, refers to thymus.) These T-cells are the body's internal radar, responsible for distinguishing between friend and foe. When they detect an invader, they become vicious fighters.

As they patrol, some of the T-cells encounter the rapidly multiplying flu virus. After checking the ID of this suspect and recognizing it to be foreign, the T-cell grabs the virus and sounds an alarm which conveys the exact identity of the invader. When the alarm sounds, the body starts to quickly reproduce more of the appropriate T-cells, which swarm to the battle site.

By this time you may be experiencing some soreness of joints or inflammation and redness of lymph nodes, sure signs that a battle is raging and the battlefield is strewn with casualties.

B-cells and Antibodies

The body next takes other white blood cells called B-cells and with the help of the thymus produces antibodies. Antibodies are uniquely and specifically prepared like guided missiles to zero in on this particular virus. Thousands are produced and released to surround the virus and hang on. Attacked from all sides by both T-cells and antibodies, the cells infected by the flu virus either suffocate or burst.

Macrophages

At this point another kind of white blood cell named the macrophage comes into action. The name macrophage means "big eater" and these cells are programed to immediately devour anything that is covered with antibodies. They arrive at the scene and begin to do their job. After they eat they may explode or at least die and become toxic. The circulatory system must perform a clean-up job and carry the remains to the elimination department.

Meanwhile, some of the antibodies are held on reserve and put into memory cells, so in case that particular virus ever approaches again, the body's defenses can respond immediately and the virus will have very little chance. Now the host has built up an immunity to that disease. This is why children seldom catch the same childhood disease twice. Since they have the needed antibodies on reserve, we say that they have developed immunity to that disease.

One might of course ask why we may get the flu several times. The answer lies in that each flu virus seems to be unique and original in its strain and design, so one must develop immunity to each strain. This is also why each flu is given a different name, often according to the place where it was first identified (for example, the Hong Kong flu).

Suppressor Cells

By this time you can realize that the immune response is so sensitive and even vicious that it will even attack the body's own

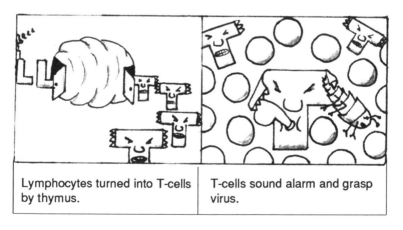

| Lymphocytes turned into T-cells by thymus. | T-cells sound alarm and grasp virus. |

cells should they turn malignant. Fortunately, there are some cells known as suppressor cells which keep this process from going too far. If these suppressor cells are not functioning adequately and the body's healthy cells are being attacked, the host is subject to autoimmune disease.

Vaccinations

In the 1790's Dr. Edward Jenner noticed that the milkmaids who had received cowpox from milking cows did not develop the more deadly smallpox. He then decided to innoculate a child with the fluid from a milkmaid's cowpox. The child escaped smallpox, having been the first person who was ever vaccinated. It was not until much later that scientists realized that this procedure activated the body's immune system to produce antibodies. These antibodies, being kept on reserve, prevented the more dreaded disease from gaining opportunity to make any significant advances.

My mother who had eight children seemed to have some intuitive insight into immunity. When one of us had one of the infectious diseases (such as mumps, measles and so on), she would have the rest of us take turns sleeping with that one. Soon after, we all had the disease and then we were all immune. Other mothers tried to isolate their children and ended up fearing and fighting that disease for years.

Mother did not understand immunity scientifically; she only knew that children seldom got the same disease twice. That

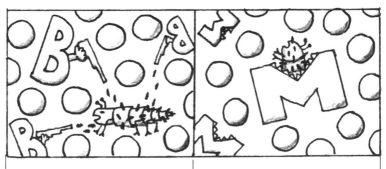

| B-cells create then fire antibodies at virus. | Macrophages eat antibody-covered virus. |

meant that once they had it, the threat was over. She noted that sometimes after a second exposure, the child might get a minor fever, but the disease would not "break out." Although she did not realize it, there were sufficient antibodies on reserve to combat the disease before it could make significant advances.

Immune Breakdown

As amazing and versatile as the immune system is, it is subject to breakdown. In an age where supersonic travel, fast food, rapid transit, cellular telephones, high pressure occupations, and jet-away vacations have become almost the standard lifestyle, the human body must withstand a great amount of stress. Add to this; chemicals in food, air and water, and travel mobility which brings one into contact with persons from every area of the globe — the stage is set for immune breakdown.

During the initial stages of a breakdown, the body indicates its distress by symptomatic reactions such as headaches, itching, rashes, fatigue, and so on. The traditional response to these symptoms is to apply chemicals and drugs both internally and externally. These add a further strain to the immune system. As if this were not enough, H.A. Huggins, D.D.S., reports that studies have shown that persons exposed to mercury will experience a reduction in the disease fighting capacity of their immune system. Yet most people today carry mercury fillings in their mouths! Is it any wonder that this overworked and underfed system sometimes cannot cope with the demands laid upon it.

Realizing the complexity of the recognition and destruction process that the immune system carries out, it is not hard to understand that this system constantly must be in top operating condition if we want to be healthy. It is also plainly obvious that if the immune system breaks down even slightly, the human body becomes ripe for enemy takeover.

If the immune system stopped functioning, it would be as though one were to walk unprotected through a hail of stray bullets. It would be just a matter of time until the fatal one hit. Consider your immune system as your bullet proof uniform and keep it in top condition. If it would stop functioning for even one day, your chances of survival would be very poor.

Autoimmune Disease

As noted earlier the lymphocytes and T-cells must detect and identify all foreign invaders and respond quickly. This demands precise and specific action with no time for hesitation and with no margin for error. Meanwhile, the suppressor cells must be always on guard to check for any undue action on friendly cells.

In the midst of this delicate check and balance system, bring in all the above-mentioned twentieth century complications, and we must marvel that the immune system can operate effectively at all. However, with the ever-quickening pace of life and the ever-increasing number of foreign substances being introduced into our body in the form of pollutants, food additives, drugs and medications, there are increasing possibilities that this balance may be disturbed. The misguided immune system then becomes its own enemy. When it has been tricked into attacking its own cells, the host becomes a victim of autoimmune disease.

Cancer

As each cell has within it the code, referred to as DNA, to replace itself both in number and in character, it is very important that this code be protected. For this protection we must again depend on the immune system. If a virus or carcinogen (any invader that has the potential to produce cancer) is allowed to break into the cell, it can distort the code and cause the cell to reproduce in an erratic, uncontrolled and mutated way. The resulting tumor may well be the beginning of the dreaded scourge of cancer.

The immune system works to protect the body from cancer in at least two ways. First, if the carcinogens are caught before they enter a cell and begin their deadly work, they can be destroyed. Second, the healthy immune system will also work to destroy the mutant, cancerous cells. This is the principle by which a revitalized immune system can sometimes defeat and even reverse the cancer process.

Ronald E. Cape, of Cetus Corp., states in *Fortune*, Feb. 2, 1987, "We now know that there is a unifying principle in cancer treatment. The principle is not the cancer itself; it is the body and its healthy reaction against abnormal cells. We've proven without any question that the immune system can be stimulated so that the body can help itself fight cancer.... We're identifying... products whose principal activity is to help the immune system do its job; and these substances are not foreign chemicals introduced into the body."

AIDS (Acquired Immune Deficiency Syndrome)

Recognized for less than a decade, this vicious killer is acknowledged by its very name to be a destroyer of the immune system. Transmitted by a virus, only through intimate contact, this minute monster knows no bounds. This virus, usually referred to as the HIV virus, is so tiny that sixteen thousand could perch on a pinhead.

Wearing a deceptive coat of protein, it eludes the advancing defenders, and zeros in on the much larger T-cell. Here, it docks itself firmly in a receptacle it finds on the T-cell membrane. Very soon it moves inside the cell, takes off its protein coat and then begins its work of taking over the cellular machinery, retooling its code so that it is now calibrated to produce more AIDS viruses. Now, this T-cell, originally a very vital part of the immune defense system, becomes an AIDS virus factory!

After multitudes of new AIDS viruses have been produced, the T-cell bursts open, spewing its malicious cargo, and thus freeing the viruses to perpetuate and repeat the process. Unless this process is arrested, the host's immune system becomes helpless, and the body is defenseless. Now, a multitude of opportunistic diseases, normally warded off by a healthy immune system, are free to attack, spreading havoc virtually unhindered. Usually, within the next months or at most within a few years the host dies.

Although it is not known whether the immune system can entirely resist or subdue the AIDS virus, obviously our immune system is our best hope should we contact this micro-mini monster.

Antibiotics and Aspirin

Robert Atkins, M.D., notes that while antibiotics are useful in bacterial infections, they are ineffective in common viral ones. Medical doctors know that most respiratory infections are viral and that viruses are self-limiting and usually go away by themselves; yet because of the patient's expectation and conditioning, they may prescribe antibiotics, nevertheless. Not only are the antibiotics often unnecessary, they frequently destroy the many helpful intestinal bacteria and deplete certain vitamins.

When antibiotics are not prescribed, aspirin is often recommended. A study by doctors at Cleveland's University Hospital has shown that aspirin compromises the infection-fighting ability of the white blood cells.

Immune Protection

If people really understood the life-protecting function of the immune system, the abuse it suffers under present day lifestyles, and the seriousness of its potential breakdown; everyone would be concerned about its protection. Yet today, millions of people suffer from frequent colds, recurring bouts of the flu, headaches, migraines, hayfever, sinus infections and allergies. All these may simply be cries of anguish from an immune system that is losing the battle against its enemies.

To stay healthy the body must create 200,000 new immune cells and thousands of antibody molecules every second. This means that millions of new cells need to be rebuilt every day. It is therefore absolutely essential that the body gets the adequate nutrients so that this defense system can stay battle-ready at all times.

We must stop looking for substances that will simply mask the symptoms of an overworked immune system and may in the long run only further overload it. Rather, let us consider some nutrients which will nourish, strengthen and supply our body's natural defense system.

Vitamins and minerals play a key role in every aspect of the immune action. According to Stuart Berger, M.D., recent research shows that a lack of **Vitamin A** lowers the number of T-cells — which means fewer immune soldiers to mount an attack.

Without enough of the **B vitamins,** particularly **B-6** and **B-12,** the cells cannot make the crucial germ-fighting antibodies.

According to Morton Walker, D.P.M., **pantothenic acid, riboflavin** and B-12 elevate the body's immune response.

Studies by Dr. Linus Pauling and others indicate that **vitamin C** strengthens the immune system. It increases the percentage of

B-lymphocyte cells and enhances immunity response. Its effect is further increased when used in conjunction with vitamin A.

All **minerals,** including the trace minerals, but especially **potassium,** have been found to be vital to immune function. Chlorophyl as found in **spirulina** has also been found to be important. Various herbs, such as **licorice root** and **echinacea** have been traditionally used for immune function.

Essential fatty acids such as in linseed oil or in **evening primrose oil** are needed to strengthen and activate the thymus and adrenal glands.

Colon Cleansing and Detoxification

Since accumulated toxins and intestinal debris can produce free radicals and add great strain on the immune system, a periodic colon cleansing program is a very important protective measure (See Chapter 4).

Consider the immune system as the army, navy, marines and air force to protect and defend the body. As these forces must be backed up by auxiliary services, so also must the immune system be backed up by body cleansing and nutritional support. Then, the human immune system will serve and protect us so we can live a long, healthy life.

An Immune System Support Program

As a natural, nutritional stimulation for the body's immune defense system, I would propose a program such as follows:

With breakfast and dinner:
Adrenal Stimulant Formula †
Beta Carotene 10,000 IU
Licorice Root 450 mg
Barley Green 700 mg
Spirulina 500 mg
Thymus substance
Evening Primrose 500 mg
Vitamin E (d-Alpha tocopherol with mixed tocopherols)

With lunch:
Adrenal substance
Chelated Minerals †
Echinacea 300 mg
Pantothenic Acid 500 mg
B-Complex
Vitamin C 500 mg
Zinc 25 mg

Chapter 6

Stepping on Candida's Uprising

If you have nagging health problems that will not go away, if you have been told by doctors that "it's all in your head and you'll have to learn to live with it;" you may be one of the many sufferers of Candida Albicans, yeast infection. In fact, according to Abram Hofer, M.D., Ph.D., "Approximately one third of our planet's population is victimized by the CANDIDA SYNDROME." Now it is time to step on the yeast.

In this chapter you will discover:

• Why yeast infection may lie at the root of many health problems.

• How symptomatic relief may actually encourage yeast overgrowth and increase health problems.

• How to recognize signs of yeast infection.

• What steps you can take to control yeast in your body.

"I had aged five years in one!"

I had been taking vitamins and minerals for years, not knowing what I should be taking, or what should be taken together. I had sinus infection with horrendous headaches. When at last I went to a doctor, he only prescribed antibiotics which depressed me and didn't help the problem. I was pale. My arms were breaking out to the elbows. I didn't feel like doing anything (a very unusual condition for me). I couldn't swim because of my sinuses. I couldn't play bridge because the headaches ruined my concentration. I had no energy for hobbies.

My husband suggested I go to a doctor. I was at crossroads. I felt like I had aged five years in one, but could I go to the doctor and let him take over my life?

I read a book on the yeast syndrome. It made sense. Then I discovered Dr. Zehr's Yeast Control Program.

I feel like a million. My headaches are gone. I'm back to gardening, golfing, and swimming in the ocean. I'm happy again!

R.L.

Health Problems of over Forty Years Eliminated

Last year I followed the Yeast Control Program for three months. I am in the process of doing it for another two months. It's amazing!

I have had yeast associated problems starting at age nine, when I developed hives. The sinus problems started at twelve. Strep throat came at 23. I took several antibiotics each time the strep appeared.

At age thirty came the allergies and hayfever. When pollen was heavy in the air, I would have to sleep sitting up. By 49, I was having problems with my muscles and joints. I spent many sleepless nights.

Thanks to the Yeast Control Program all of these problems have been eliminated. I am so grateful because I had looked many places for answers but found none. I have also followed the Body Cleansing and Detoxification Program and am also very grateful for it.

Thank you Dr. Zehr for these programs.

A.R.

Clients Helped to Conceive

For several years now I have been helping many clients who have been trying for years to get pregnant. Although I use kinesiology balancing as well, I feel that the Yeast Control Program, herbal combination for female irregularities, and ovarian nucleoprotein substance are instrumental in helping my clients conceive.

In fact, now when I suggest these, I warn my clients to take the necessary precautions if they don't want to expand their family!

S.R.

"If you suffer from **acne, allergies, anxiety, asthma, constipation, depression..., fatigue, headaches..., persistent coughs, premenstrual syndrome, recurrent vaginitis, skin irritations** you may be a victim of THE YEAST SYNDROME," John Parks Trowbridge, M.D., and Morton Walker, D.P.M.

"They may say you're neurotic, but...do you experience...**depression, anxiety, irrational irritability, bloating...** In men, women and children these may be the symptoms of a correctable illness — chronic CANDIDIASIS..." *The Missing Diagnosis,* C. Orian Truss, M.D.

"A weakened immune system, subjected to poor diet, antibiotics or lifestyle, is an open invitation to Candida albicans 'population explosion' and expansion. The invading yeast organism can go almost anywhere in the body and do almost anything, for example it can cause **asthma, chronic bronchitis...**" *Candida: A Twentieth Century Disease,* Shirley S. Lorenzani, Ph.D.

CANDIDA — What is it?

Candida albicans is a specific form of yeast which is found in the human body, especially in the digestive tract, bronchials and vagina. Yeast are single cell fungus which are always determined to spread, but are normally kept under control by a non-polluted healthy body with a strong immune system. If it is given opportunity to spread, it begins to choke and frustrate the normal function of the body. This produces many symptoms, yet most treatments for these symptoms only compound the problem.

The human body has an amazing built-in capacity to protect, defend and maintain itself. This vital function is performed by what is referred to as the body's immune system. Good nutrition, clean environment and adequate rest should guarantee good health and normal body function for the average human. But in the last century, it seems that something has gone wrong. Health breakdown, instead of being the fate of an unfortunate few, is becoming the lot of many.

The Complaint

People all over are becoming more and more frustrated in their search for better health. Almost every day we hear statements like the following: I don't know when it all started and I'm not sure what's wrong, but I just don't feel the way I know I should. Oh yes, I've talked to lots of doctors and many well-meaning friends, and I've tried everything from diet to drugs. Sometimes I think I'm gaining, but overall it seems I'm gradually getting worse.

Deep coughing leads to bronchitis. Antibiotics seem to beat it temporarily, but it always comes back. There seems to be no end to exhaustion, lack of energy, easy infections, frequent colds, and an ever-increasing number of allergic reactions. Do I really have to learn to live with it? Is this my future? Or is there really some little critter inside me who's giving me a hard time? When I ask my doctor about Candida albicans he just smiles. The problem is he hasn't helped me and although he is smiling, I'm not! Is there any help out there?

The Complication

Although there have been great advances in this century, the body has not been fully able to adapt to new pressures from chemicals and toxic pollutants in air, food and water. It is beginning to complain. These complaints take the form of headaches, rashes, aches, skin eruptions, cramps, congestion, bloating, persistent coughs, excessive fatigue, and so on. All of these are symptoms. Symptoms are acknowledged to be "evidence of something not seen."

Symptoms such as the above mentioned are uncomfortable; hence, the normal response is to seek relief. This quest for relief has inspired scientists to concoct countless chemical potions. These potions when dispensed by highly trained practitioners have earned the respect of all sufferers, and are injected, ingested and inhaled into human bodies by the train-car load.

Since symptomatic relief is what we seek, that is what we get. Unfortunately, however, that is not all we get. To put a gag on the messenger who brings the bad news is not necessarily the long term answer. Why try to choke the messenger? Why not deal with the real problem?

Even under ideal conditions the body's immune system is busily engaged in regulating and controlling the body's internal bacteria and fungi. But today, it must exist in an environment where pollution in air, food, and water overload its immunization capacity. When it sends forth distress signals in the form of symptoms, our health care system pours on the wonder drugs and chemicals. While there may be some sense of temporary symptomatic relief, the body's vital immune system is further harassed. Before long it cannot maintain its crucial role of keeping bacteria, yeast and fungi under control. The yeast such as Candida albicans being an opportunistic fungus is free to perform its damaging conquests. The stage is now set for the YEAST SYNDROME!

The Disease — CANDIDIASIS

The Fungus Kingdom

The body we live in is also the home of countless other inhabitants who claim the right to live, multiply and die. If allowed to, these inhabitants would like to take over completely. These microorganisms belong to the fungus kingdom, and if kept in check seem to coexist with us. However, in recent years one of their tribes known as Candida albicans has become more aggressive.

Although we might wish that the fungus kingdom did not exist, it does serve a valuable function. Fungi speed up decay, and process organic material, so that it decomposes, becomes soil and can be reused. If there were no fungi, the remains of all plants and animals that ever existed would still be with us!

Since the work of fungi is inevitable, we have no choice, but the issue becomes more crucial when they attempt to digest our body before we move out! Although we may not feel or hear the teeth gnawing, Candida may be killing us softly, while its population increases and its troops range further afield to spread its civilization into more organs of our body.

The Immune System

Although the fungus known as Candida albicans seems to be found to some extent in all human beings, it is ,nevertheless, foreign to the body. Because of this, the body reacts to it in the same way that it reacts to viruses and bacteria. Our body's ability to cope with the illnesses induced by such infectious agents depends very much on our body's immune system.

Certain of the body's white cells are the most important factors in the immune warfare. They are sometimes referred to as B cells. These cells must also be able to recognize the body's own constituents so that they do not attack their own. To avoid such an attack, we have further specialized white blood cells called suppressor cells. If these fail we may react to our own tissue. This is referred to as autoimmune disease.

In addition to the B cells, other blood cells referred to as T cells also play a vital role in the body's defense system. These are white blood cells turned into T cells by hormones from the thymus and are also known as lymphocytes. They control certain blood cells by commanding them to destroy bacteria and kill foreign invaders in the body.

Foreign substances to which the immune system responds are known as antigens. Candida albicans has many antigens, but the strength of the immune response to the antigens depends on the vigor and vitality of the host's immune system.

When the immune response is inadequate, the invading germ will not be destroyed, but rather will be allowed to multiply and pervade the tissues of the body. This fungus, existing in the tissues, releases toxic yeast products into the host's system and results in the symptoms common to CANDIDIASIS.

If the immune system can regain its ability to deal with the yeast infection, then the fungus will be eliminated from the tissues and will no longer release its damaging products into the bloodstream. Then, the symptoms should disappear.

From the above it can be realized that any foreign matter introduced into the body whether by food, air or injection, can place a heavy burden on the body's defense system. This is why medications, drugs and antibiotics, although administered as "health care" can actually promote health destruction. This is also why tobacco, alcohol, coffee and other "vices" take their toll in weakening the body's vitality.

The Reason — Popular Lifestyle Instigates Health Breakdown

Consider the complications of the popular lifestyle of today's average person and also consider the demand each aspect puts on the body.

1. Living in the Fast Lane! Constant movement, super-sonic travel, fast food, stress and pressure, evening activities, and minimum rest.

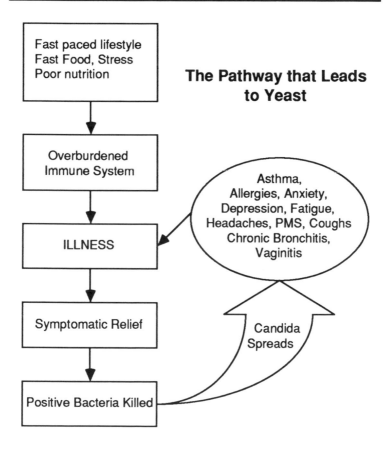

The Pathway that Leads to Yeast

Fast paced lifestyle Fast Food, Stress Poor nutrition

Overburdened Immune System

ILLNESS

Asthma, Allergies, Anxiety, Depression, Fatigue, Headaches, PMS, Coughs Chronic Bronchitis, Vaginitis

Symptomatic Relief

Candida Spreads

Positive Bacteria Killed

Result: Stress and tension on the body require extra nutrition, but fast food supplies only the minimum, and by its "on-the-go" nature minimizes digestion. Coffee and other caffeine beverages toxify the body. Donuts and sugar of all kinds supply empty calories and feed yeast overgrowth. Lack of rest, relaxation, and reflection rob the body of much needed opportunity to restore, repair and rebuild blood and vital tissue. Gradually the body weakens, virus and bacteria take advantage, and numerous symptoms appear.

2. Seeking Symptomatic Relief. With no time and no interest in understanding the body's symptomatic reactions, immediate relief is demanded. In response to this demand, myriads of drugs and medications have been formulated. These interfere and intervene in the body's normal function.

Result: The real problem is not addressed; the body's normal function is frustrated; and further pressure is put on the already overburdened immune system. Many times the immune system is fully engaged in trying to combat this foreign invasion.

3) Needing Antibiotics. With the immune system exhausted, the person becomes subject to viral illnesses, easy infection, bronchitis, colds and flu. The unquestioned antidote for most all of these problems is more and more antibiotics.

Result: The antibiotics being unselective will kill not only virus, but also positive bacteria which are needed for digestion and for the control of yeast.

4. Candida explosion! Candida albicans, normally confined to the large intestine, seizes the opportunity and spreads to the vagina, throat, ears and even into the bloodstream.

Result: The host becomes easily tired, irritable and even more susceptible to disease. Symptoms multiply, the immune system is overloaded, allergies appear, more medication is prescribed, and the YEAST SYNDROME is in action.

Recognition — How Do I Know If I Have It?

Since Candida organisms are usually present on everyone's mucous membranes, including the mouth, digestive tract, and the vagina, skin tests and cultures are of little help in diagnosis. The accepted diagnosis is based on the ratings you give your own health. If, for example, you can identify with at least ten of the conditions in the following list, you probably would benefit from treatment to control yeast infection:

frequent infection	poor concentration	breath shortness
skin problems	painful joints	easy bruising
fatigue	dry mouth or throat	birth control pills
no energy	nose congestion	frequent colds
irritability	headaches	dry scaly skin
craving for sweets	chest pains	vaginal itch or burning
allergic reactions	dark circles under the eyes	
digestion problems	periodic antibiotic treatment	
bloating	tired of doctor-to-doctor shopping.	
bad breath		

For a more complete list to help you further evaluate your condition, see some of the books listed in Appendix D.

The Correction

To correct this complex disorder, a number of steps must be taken:

1. Yeast overgrowth must be destroyed.

The yeast which has converted itself into fungus and is rooted into the walls of the intestine is not about to retreat without a battle. Although this battle may be waged by drugs, they will often simply prolong the syndrome. Natural source caprylic acid, garlic and certain herbs are much more compatible with healthy body function. Biotin has also been found to inhibit the conversion of the yeast to its harmful fungous form.

2. The damage caused must be repaired.

When the yeast "die-off" takes place, it becomes toxic. Garlic, vitamin C, vitamin A and vitamin E may help to reduce infection. The fungus having rooted into the intestines will leave pockets, known as rhizoids. Chlorophyl can help to heal the damaged mucous membranes that line the colon.

3. Positive bacteria must be replenished.

The positive bacteria, lactobacillus, which is necessary for "nutrient processing" in the large intestine and which has been depleted can be restored by a generous supply of acidophilus.

4. The immune system must be strengthened.

An abundant supply of the vital nutrients such as pantothenic acid and thymus substance can aid in strengthening and activating the immune system.

5. Lifestyle must be adjusted.

From the above it can be realized that lifestyle; particularly diet, health care, and stress; sets the stage for Candidiasis, so it becomes imperative that these areas be adjusted in order to avoid a re-occurrence of the problem.

Avoid — All forms of sugar, including such as found in donuts,cereals, catsup, syrups, sweetened juices, jams, cookies, molasses, ice cream, shakes, etc.

— Alcoholic beverages, coffee, tea (except herbal teas)

— All yeast-containing foods, baked goods, pastries, cantaloupes, mushrooms, dried fruits, cheeses (except cottage cheese and unsweetened yogurt)

— Processed meats, sausages, bacon, corned beef, ham

— Pickled foods, salad dressings and old leftovers

Limited Amounts of: Unsweetened juices, fresh fruit, nuts, peanut butter, grains, cottage cheese, yogurt

Freely Eat — Vegetables (preferably raw or steamed), eggs, meat, fish, fowl, lamb, beef, brown rice

Avoid — Antibiotics if possible, use supplements, herbs, and natural health-aids

Take time to sit down to eat, chew your food, relax, exercise, and get adequate rest. The returns in better health, a renewed sense of well-being, and increased productivity will be well worth the extra time!

A Yeast Control Program

A comprehensive nutritional yeast control program should last two to three months and must follow the five-fold attack outlined above.

The following program of supplements has been designed to take care of the first four points:

In the morning:

Acidophilus (1 billion) Vitamin C (500 mg)
Caprylic Acid (300 mg) Thymus Nucleoprotein
Biotin (300 mcg) substance
Chlorophyl enriched alfalfa (350 mg)

In the afternoon:
2 Multi Vitamin Mineral †
Beta Carotene (10,000 I.U.)
Poke Root or Taheebo
Vitamin E with mixed
    tocopherols
Linseed Oil (340 mg)
Pantothenic Acid (500 mg)
Vitamin C (500 mg)

In the evening:
Acidophilus (1 billion)
Caprylic Acid (300 mg)
Biotin (300 mcg)
Chlorophyl enriched
    alfalfa (350 mg)
Garlic (2 capsules)

For best results, I suggest taking the morning supplements on an empty stomach between breakfast and lunch; take the afternoon supplements with the main meal of the day; and take the evening supplements at bedtime, preferably on an empty stomach.

The intensity of this program may activate some definite body responses. Mild headache may indicate heavy toxicity being removed from the body. Stomach uneasiness may indicate weak digestion; try adding Digestive Enzyme Supplement. Some stomach or abdominal discomfort is normal, as the yeast-kill will generate some toxicity. If strong discomfort persists, eliminate the Poke Root. Continue on the program and try to re-introduce half the Poke Root after several days. If the discomfort continues after the Poke Root has been removed, cut Caprylic Acid consumption in half in the morning and evening. Re-introduce as it can be tolerated.

Dietary discretion is very important. Follow the guidelines described earlier.

I would recommend a minimum of two months on this program. Three to four months may be needed for full control to be attained.

Chapter 7

Stepping Out of Chronic Fatigue Syndrome

In recent years a new mysterious health affliction has been identified. While experts cannot agree on its name, those who feel like they have a permanent case of the flu know it is real.

Dr. Paul Donald has said, "If it weren't for AIDS, Chronic Epstein-Barr virus syndrome (CEBVS) would be the disease of the decade."

If
- you need much more sleep than usual and are still tired
- rest and sleep still leave you in a state of fatigue
- muscles are weak and aching after very little use
- you can't remember, lose attention, say the wrong word
- depression, anxiety and personality changes increase
- flu-like illnesses, and chronic sore throats become recurrent

Then
don't let them tell you
- you're crazy, neurotic, it's all in your head
- your job probably doesn't agree with you — better change it
- a positive mental attitude can help to overcome anything
- some people just normally feel tired, weak and achey

It's time
- to learn the facts
- to take control
- to overcome the mystery disease with many names

Mononucleosis Dragged On

As a very active 21 year-old I was more than a little disappointed when I was hit by a severe case of mononucleosis a little over a year ago. I rested. I took lots of supplements, but I just couldn't beat it. I felt like I was sleeping my life away. One of my weekly highlights was stepping onto the front porch! Over time, I did improve enough to sleepwalk through a fraction of the things that had formerly been my normal routine.

I've been following Dr. Zehr's program for four months. I am happy to report that I am now fully back in action!

M.F.

This mysterious ailment has been given many different names. Some of them are as follows:

CFIDS (Chronic Fatigue and Immune Dysfunction Syndrome)
CFS (Chronic Fatigue Syndrome)
CEBVS (Chronic Epstein-Barr Virus Syndrome)
M.E. (Myalgic Encephalomyelitis)
Epidemic Neuromyasthenia
Iceland Disease
Lake Tahoe Disease
"Yuppie Flu"

So What is This Mystery Disease?

Generally speaking, CFIDS, as we shall call it, is a complex illness characterized by extreme fatigue, neurological problems, and symptoms that can resemble a persistent case of mononucleosis. The victim often finds herself in a state of utter exhaustion with extremely poor stamina. These symptoms tend to wax and wane but are often severely debilitating and may last for months or even years. While all ages are at risk, adults under age 45 seem to be the most susceptible with the majority being women. The typical victim is one who has been generally quite active and has enjoyed good health in the past.

The Epstein-Barr virus was discovered in 1964, but it took twenty years for people to realize that its effects could be so long lasting. In the fall of 1984 the small town of Incline Village, Nevada found a surprising number of its residents falling victim to a sudden rash of flu-like symptoms such as: profound fatigue, prolonged sore throat, swollen glands, and sore muscles. With the flu these symptoms might have remained for up to two weeks but in these cases they seemed to persist almost endlessly. This was more than an extended bout with the flu, it was a mysterious seemingly endless battle with debilitating exhaustion.

Blood tests in many cases found a high level of Epstein-Barr virus (EBV) antibodies, suggesting active EBV infection. Researchers suddenly realized the seriousness of the disease; hence, the C was added to change the designation to chronic Epstein-Barr virus (CEBV). Since then, many people in many places who had been suffering as much from misunderstanding as from disease have been found to be victims of the "mystery disease."

What Causes CFIDS?

Since the research and understanding of this complex problem are just developing, it is hard to answer this question fully. We do know that this is a viral disease associated with the dysfunction of the immune system. It was thought that the Epstein-Barr virus which causes mononucleosis also caused the syndrome. However, although many CFIDS patients have high levels of EBV antibodies which indicate the presence of the EBV, it is now felt that EBV may be a result of CFIDS rather than the cause. This would explain the mononucleosis like symptoms. In the search to find the cause, other agents are now being considered, such as HHV-6 (a mysterious new virus), other herpes viruses, enteroviruses, retroviruses, or other yet undiscovered agents. In any case, we do know that a weakened immune system greatly increases the possibility of being victimized.

If the host has a high resistance level and his immune function is strong, even though he may be carrying the virus, it will have little opportunity to inflict disease.

What are the Symptoms?

CFIDS is an individualistic disease, so symptoms vary greatly. However, the following are the most commonly reported, in order of percentage frequency.

Fatigue	100
Headaches	83

Depression	78
Sleep disturbance	73
Poor memory/concentration	65
Sore throat	63
Muscle aches/pains	60
Swollen lymph glands	55
Joint pains	45
Weight loss	22
Rash	10

Further symptoms may include visual disturbances such as blurring, sensitivity to light, and eye pain; psychological problems such as anxiety, panic attacks, chills and night sweats; shortness of breath; dizziness and balance problems; menstrual problems; chest pains; increased allergies; and sensitivities to odors and chemicals.

While any one of these by itself does not suggest CFIDS, if over half of the "top ten" are in evidence, it is probable that this disease may be in process.

In recent years a number of organizations have been established to research this illness. Journals and a lot of helpful information can be obtained by contacting these. Two such organizations are:

In Canada:
    M.E. Canada
    400 - 246 Queen St.
    Ottawa, ON K1P 5E4

In the United States:
    CFIDS Society, Inc.
    P.O. Box 230108
    Portland, OR 97223

Possible Responses

Since this is a viral assault on the body there are three possible responses.

1. Normal Immune Response. The immune system responds homeostatically, trying to correct the imbalance and return everything to a normal and balanced state. This is the normal way that most people resist the CFIDS threats. However, for a good number, the attack is so overwhelming that outside help is needed.

2. Drug Therapy. Drugs are hyperpurified "dead" substances that act directly and specifically on the disease process itself,

rather than strengthen the body's natural defenses against disease. There are no drugs presently known to be effective against CFIDS. Besides, to introduce another invader is to put more stress on the body, which is hardly needed.

3. Immune Support. We can stimulate the immune system to a heightened level of competence that will not merely beat back the virus but will leave the body more resistant to disease in general. This approach uses agents such as diet, exercise, vitamin supplements, enzymes and herbal compounds.

Some of the elements found to be most effective in this approach include: beta carotene, barley green, calcium, magnesium, echinacea, co-enzyme Q10, evening primrose oil, folic acid, pantothenic acid, selenium and zinc.

The following proposed program brings together a carefully blended spectrum of the nutrients which are reported to have some positive effect in treating this disease. While this program is relatively new, the test results and reports of a number of persons who are following it have been very encouraging.

In the morning and evening take:
Beta Carotene (10,000 I.U.)
Vitamin B12 (500 mcg)
Calcium Pangamate (B15)
Calcium (300 mg) with Magnesium (150 mg)
Coenzyme Q10 (10 mg)
Echinacea (300 mg)
1 Multi Vitamin Mineral †

At noon take:
Barley Green (700 mg)
B Complex
Vitamin E (d-alpha tocopherol with mixed tocopherols)
Evening Primrose Oil (500 mg)
Folic Acid (10 mg)
Pantothenic Acid (500 mg)
Selenium (100 mcg)
Zinc (25 mg)

Chapter 8

Keeping Nature's Balance in Weight Control

According to the United States Department of Public Health, over 80 million Americans are more than 20 percent overweight and as many as 75 percent of all adult Americans may be at least ten pounds overweight.

Although countless diets and weight loss plans have been heralded as the solution to this weighty dilemma, in most cases the long term loss is in the victim's pocketbook and the gain is mostly in the marketeer's bank account. Unless the victim of obesity is helped to realize and understand how the body is handling or mishandling food, and how cooperating with the body can bring about normal weight control, permanent results can never be achieved.

In this chapter you will discover:

• What are the underlying causes of overweight and obesity.

• Why typical diets and weight loss schemes usually only provide temporary help at best.

• How your body's weight is a reaction to environmental and "invironmental" factors.

•What you can do to assist your body to balance and control your weight.

"I had tried everything."

For twenty-five years I've been trying to lose weight and I've tried every diet on the market. None of them worked. After thirty days on Dr. Zehr's Weight Control Program I had lost one size and I felt fantastic. Almost everyone I met was complimenting me on how good I looked.

What I like about this program is that it taught me how to control my weight. Now, before I dine out, I take the evening supplements to suppress my appetite and help me digest my food. If I know I'll be eating a big meal in the evening, I take the noon supplements and protein powder at lunch.

I'm not waiting to gain weight so I can lose it again. I'm controlling my weight.

A..D.

"I was skeptical."

I've always been very healthy and very cynical about vitamins and so forth. I did, however, have the desire to lose some weight. Finally, I agreed to go on Dr. Zehr's Weight Control Program. I felt wonderful! I had more energy, less hunger and less stress than when I was eating "normally." In the first month I lost ten pounds. In the second month I lost another ten.

Keeping the weight off has been no problem because the program changed my eating habits. I'm more careful about what I eat. I eat more fruit than before, and I drink much more water.

G.W.

Weight Control Is Different From Weight Loss

A proper weight control program must harmonize with the body's basic functions, remove the obstacles, and meet the body's total need. Such a program will assist the body to function at its desired state of normalcy. Remember, given the proper opportunity, the body will always move toward normal good health and normal body weight.

Weight loss, dieting and other schemes for reducing weight are all frustrating to the body's *status quo* functioning. At best, they are ways which can give temporary symptomatic relief. Since they neither harmonize with the body's chemistry, nor address the person's real problem, they usually end in frustration and failure as anyone who has tried them will readily affirm.

The Underlying Problems

Overweight or obesity is not the basic problem. It is merely a symptom of other problems. When we address the real problems, the symptom we call overweight will take care of itself normally and naturally. Let us look at the four underlying health problems and consider how they affect obesity.

1. Toxicity

Given the present environment and normal food intake, it is inevitable that the human body will pick up and carry a great amount of toxicity and accumulated waste materials. This makes normal body function very difficult and puts much stress on digestion, assimilation, absorption, and metabolism. A normal response to this stress is for the body to accumulate fat tissue in order to protect itself from accumulating toxicity.

2. Inefficiency

A further problem arising from toxicity, accumulated waste and mucus is that the body becomes very inefficient in its chemistry of food use. Refined carbohydrates, fats, and other calorie-laden foods will be easily and quickly utilized. Proteins, enzymes, minerals, and other "solid" foods will be poorly absorbed, so that even though caloric intake may be in excess of the body's normal needs, the body will still express hunger because its needs are not being met. In fact, while excess calories are being translated into fat cells, the body may be unable to absorb a sufficient supply of other nutrients and thus may still be "starving" for adequate nutrition. This sets the stage for overeating. Such a condition quite naturally leads to overweight. Yet, eating less is not the complete answer.

3. Bad Nutrition

The human body is obligated to use whatever it is given. Unfortunately for some of us, we are what we have been eating. The body cannot change junk food into good nutrition. A diet high in refined carbohydrates and fats will also further decrease the body's digestive efficiency. Each of the above factors sets the stage which makes obesity almost inevitable.

4. Attitude and Appestat

Another problem usually underlying overweight is attitude. The attitude has probably been damaged through abuse by parents or peers, or by frequent failure in trying to lose weight. This may have brought the person to a demoralized state of convinced incapacity. In this state of mind, the victim is fully convinced that "I'll always be fat so there is no hope for change."

An area related to this is the appestat. Experiments have shown that when a certain part of the brain of a rat is damaged, the animal will starve to death with no sense of hunger. It is this part of the brain that is the seat of the appestat. The appestat is the indicator of hunger, need and satisfaction. If we are toxic and our food use is inefficient, it is likely that our appestat is presently calibrated to demand excessive volumes of food.

Dealing with the Problems

Having observed the basic underlying problems related to overweight, we will now address each one. In each case we will consider how we can work in harmony with the body's function and chemistry to address each of the underlying problems. Each point is a logical and natural step toward arriving at and maintaining normal body weight.

1. TOXICITY calls for DETOXIFICATION

While there are various programs for detoxification, a very convenient and effective one is described in Chapter Four. That program has been used successfully by thousands of people. If you have not been on such a program within the last six months, it is strongly recommended that you begin there and follow the directions as closely as possible.

During the Body Cleansing and Detoxification Program, many of the frustrations to weight control will be removed and the body will be ready for further steps. Most people begin to lose weight just by detoxifying.

It is also very important to remember that drinking lots of water is a great detoxifier. Make a strong decision that drinking lots of water will become a normal part of your natural lifestyle. If you do not enjoy drinking water, it is probably because the water is polluted. I would urge you to get a water purification system or buy bottled water. Your health deserves it.

2. From INEFFICIENCY to EFFICIENCY

The Body Cleansing and Detoxification Program will greatly assist in dealing with this problem. Removing mucus from the small intestine and the encrustment from the colon wall will allow much greater efficiency, and you will find yourself less hungry because assimilation will be improved. Digestion will also improve. Your body's efficiency will be further developed as you move into the Weight Control Program outlined at the end of this chapter.

Another way to increase the body's overall efficiency is exercise. Although there are many effective exercise programs, it is not necessary to get into one that is complicated. Many have discovered walking to be a natural, normal exercise. Every day exercise your will to walk. The secret key to any exercise program is consistency. In other words, keep doing it!

As you exercise your will to walk and to drink more water, you *will* control your weight.

3. From BAD NUTRITION to PROPER EATING

While I am not about to propose a "big diet deal," we will need to learn to eat right. Since the result will be feeling right, and looking right, and since I will guide you into eating right, this will be an easy hurdle.

In the past, your body has been conditioned to a certain way of eating and will insist on it unless directed otherwise. This idea will be easier to accept if the body's needs are fully met, and if proper eating is put forward in an orderly and acceptable form. At this point, following the Weight Control Program is most crucial. This program will meet the needs of your body. As you follow it, it will "re-train" your body to find complete satisfaction in a normal way and so be released from the frustrations which have resulted in overweight. After three to six months of following this program and experiencing its effect both on weight and body function, it will become a comfortable, normal routine. By this time your "normal way of life" will allow your body to control its weight naturally.

4. ATTITUDE — "I can" and APPESTAT — "you will"

The above factors will activate the necessary physical adjustments and bring the body into a condition where it is able to deal with the problems which result in overweight. It must, however, have the full cooperation of the will; otherwise the result will be uncomfortable and probably only temporary. The word "control" in the phrase "weight control" does imply that some attitudinal effort is involved. It suggests that the candidate is willing to exercise a certain amount of determination. The strength for this determination is born out of a clear understanding of how logical it is to work with our body rather than against it. Basic necessary attitudinal factors include: a belief that this approach is logical and possible; and a willingness to take reasonable and normal steps to manage our appetite. As we take command of our feelings, our appestat will "reprogram" itself to harmonize with the renewed dynamics of our body and we will find that the problem of appetite becomes quite manageable.

Applying the Principles of Weight Control and Body Balance

The Basic Concept

Although this approach is very logical, it is very important to clearly understand the concept. In this section I assume that you are clear about the points presented thus far. What follows is the practical application of this concept.

Overweight is a result and a symptom of four basic problems which do not allow the body to function normally and efficiently. When these problems are understood and taken care of, the body will control weight in a normal healthy way. The four problems developed earlier in this chapter, toxicity, inefficiency, bad nutrition, and attitude/appestat, will be corrected as you follow the steps outlined below. If you are experiencing a weight control problem, it is recommended that you follow this weight control program for a minimum of four months.

Step #1. Attitude - "Get Set!"

Our physical body is responsive to our mental attitude. If you have battled with weight control, your attitude and belief that a change is possible may be negative. The success of this program is based on a belief that you will succeed, and that you have the determination to make it work. This step will not be difficult when the unique and logical philosophy of this approach is understood. Study and become familiar with the concepts as outlined earlier until you "see it" and believe it, then determine that you can and will lose weight. Success will be yours!

Step # 2. Detoxification — Get Cleansed

Toxicity from air, water, food, and environment accumulate in the body. This frustrates the body's metabolism, and greatly decreases its efficiency of food use. If you have not gone through the Body Cleansing and Detoxification Program within the past six weeks, do it now as the first step to weight control!

Water is an effective daily cleanser. Let me recommend that hot water, warm water and cool water are all preferable to ice water. Ice water chills the digestive system and frustrates digestion when taken with food. Start now to make water a part of your daily routine:

- One glass of water in the morning at least 15 minutes before breakfast.
- One glass one or two hours after breakfast.
- One glass one half hour before lunch.
- One glass one or two hours after lunch.
- One glass one half hour before dinner.
- At least one or two glasses one hour after dinner.

Note: Keep liquids to a minimum during meal time. Herbal teas are okay, but ice water is a no-no.

Step # 3. Proper Eating — Get Balanced!

For this step see the instructions with the suggested weight control program described at the end of the chapter.

1. Easy on the calories — they must be either burned or collected. If you do not want to burn or collect them, do not swallow them! This does not mean count calories, but it does mean, use your good sense. Be calorie wise. For example, an egg and a slice of white bread both contain about 75 calories. However, the slice of white bread does not have enough nutrients to sustain a mouse, whereas the egg is rich in nutrients and protein. Also, remember that since all forms of sugars and fats are loaded with calories but empty of nutrition; they will add weight while robbing your body of health.

2. Water, water, water — water is your best helper. Drink as indicated earlier. Often when you feel hungry your body is just asking for water. A refreshing drink of water will often meet the need. Water can also make you feel and look better.

3. Walk, walk, walk — walking is a normal and natural exercise. Take at least one long walk (over 15 minutes) every other day. Dream up new ways of walking and new places to walk to. Why pay for and then blow exercise resolutions when you can walk? Walk away from obesity and on to vibrant health.

4. Super snacks — the great snacks are: water, "singing," raw veggies, fresh fruit, popcorn, and rice cakes. Who could ask for anything more? Enjoy them freely and with good conscience. They will make a healthier, happier you!

Step #4. Attitude and Appestat — "Get Controlled!"

Weight loss will be the normal result of following the above steps. The real goal is to maintain the weight level which you and your body agree is comfortable and normal for you. For the control that this requires, consider the following:

1. Yes, I can! — Determine now that without a doubt you can and will succeed. Set modest and realistic goals and then see how much you can exceed your goals.

2. See the why of the negative and of the positive — To understand and visualize why things are good or bad for you allows you to apply your will on a logical basis. Good and bad are not a matter of like and dislike but of what something is and what it does to me. Dramatically visualize these relationships:

The Negative Side		The Positive side	
processed		alive	
fried		raw	
sweet	= fat and fatigue	fresh	= health and energy
greasy		natural	
fat		whole	

For positive results, let us keep on the positive side.

3. Believe your inner sense — Your inner sense will tell you what is good for you and what is not. It may tell you that you have had enough before your plate is empty. Verbally confirm what your sense is telling you and then *don't empty your plate!* Your body wants to be normal and will help you if you listen. When you sense your body saying, "that's too much" or "that's not good for me," speak that feeling out loud. Then obey it.

4. Re-train your appestat — Your appestat may be somewhat of a spoiled brat! Make it your student, not your master. Teach it how to listen to your body. Gradually you can bring your appetite in line with your real needs and requirements. This will take some discipline and maybe a few lectures to yourself, but will be a crucial factor in your success.

5. Don't watch the scales or the clock — The way you feel, the way you look, and the new sizes of the clothes you wear are more important than the numbers on a scale. Besides, muscle weighs more than fat. Watching the clock move toward mealtime teases the appestat. When you notice that it is still an hour before meal time, ocupy yourself with something. Then, the time will pass more quickly and the "hunger" will fade away. If you think you are hungry, drink a glass of water. If ten minutes later you are still hungry, it is probably real.

6. "Fall" Forward — If you experience apparent failures, assess them carefully and learn from them. These can become stepping stones for your future success. Even a "fall" is of value if you learn something from it. This is what I call "falling forward."

7. Savor your success — To attain a goal is great but to maintain it is a deep and character-building experience. Discipline is the basis for success. This success will become the platform from which you will be able to reach many more of your personal goals. Congratulations! You can succeed with a purely natural weight control program, by balancing your body for healthy living!

A Natural Weight Control
and Body Balancing Program

Here is a suggested program with contents and instructions for use. I would recommend that it be followed for a minimum of four months. While following this program, daily remind yourself of and follow the principles already outlined.

Instructions

Continue this program for a minimum of four months or until weight control has been established as a normal life pattern.

With your **morning meal** you need a balanced supply of supplementary nutrients. Take:
1 Multi Vitamin Mineral†
Calcium (300 mg) Magnesium (150 mg)
Vitamin E (d-Alpha tocopherol with mixed tocopherols)
Selenium (100 mcg)
Calcium Pangamate (B15) (100 mg)

One half hour **before your noon meal** take the following supplements with eight ounces of water to suppress the appetite, help the body burn excess fat and provide fiber:
2 Oat bran fiber tablets
Kelp
Vitamin B-6 (10 mg)
Apple Cider Vinegar
2 High fiber "filler" capsules

As your **noon meal** take one serving of a high quality, vitamin enriched protein powder with either skim milk or water.

One half hour **before your evening meal** take the following supplements with eight ounces of water to suppress the appetite, help the body burn excess fat and provide fiber:
2 Oat bran fiber tablets
Kelp
Vitamin B-6 (10 mg)
Apple Cider Vinegar
2 High fiber "filler" capsules

With your **evening meal** take the following to provide nutritional and digestive elements:
1 Multi Vitamin Mineral†
Vitamin C (500 mg)
Iron (35 mg)
1 Digestive Enzyme Supplement†
Zinc (25 mg)

Chapter 9

Steps to
Reverse Heart Disease

Today the words *heart attack* strike fear in the ears of those who hear. Heart disease and stroke cause more deaths per year in the U.S.A. and Canada than all other causes of death combined, including cancer. Present statistics show that in the U.S.A. and Canada well over 1,100,000 people die of heart disease every year. That is about 3,000 people per day.

Nearly half of these victims are stricken in the prime years of their lives. To add to the gloom is the fact that while in 1900 this problem was very rare, its occurrence is now increasing at an alarming rate.

As the ancient plague demanded positive action in environmental sanitation, so the modern plague demands drastic steps to deal with internal sanitation.

In this chapter you will discover:

• Why lowering cholesterol may not be enough to save you from heart disease.

• What the root cause of heart disease is and how it develops inside you.

• Why traditional treatment for heart disease is so often ineffective.

• How to recognize when your heart is crying for help.

• What steps you can take to help your body fight heart disease.

Troubled by Varicose Veins

I was troubled by varicose veins for years. My doctor suggested stripping my veins but being a nurse, and not a very brave one, I let it go. After one month on Dr. Zehr's Oral Chelation program, the pressure in my calf has disappeared and my veins are slowly but surely disappearing also. This certainly is a wonderful option to surgery.

B.S.

Heart Disease Runs in Family

Heart disease runs in my family and blood pressure has always been a problem with me. After following Dr. Zehr's Oral Chelation Program for three months, the ringing in my ears stopped, my blood pressure decreased, and I had a greater sense of well-being. After a second three month period, I no longer get cold feet and the varicose veins in my leg are almost unnoticeable.

D.F.

Saved from By-Pass Surgery

Almost eight years ago my father had double by-pass surgery. Ever since the surgery, he could hardly work. He could also only walk a short distance before getting exhausted. The doctors told him that he would never be able to work full time again. A year ago he was told that he would have to have another by-pass surgery. One day, after almost passing out while driving, he decided to try the Oral Chelation Program.

After two months he began to notice a difference. Today, he is working full time and has lots of energy. The last time he went to his doctor, he received a clean bill of health.

G. V.

What Is Really Going On

To understand what triggers heart attack we must realize that most heart attacks come from a disease called atherosclerosis. Atherosclerosis is characterized by a waxy buildup of plaque on the walls of blood vessels. When this plaque buildup involves the coronary vessels, the ones that supply the heart muscle itself, the stage is set for a heart attack.

A major, and often first, symptom of this condition may be a chest pain called angina pectoris which in Latin means simply "pain in the chest." This pain is a symptom and is not the disease. Angina which is also referred to as coronary insufficiency occurs when one or more of the coronary arteries is narrowed or is in a spasm. A spasm is a sudden, abnormal and involuntary contracting of a muscle or group of muscles. At such a time, the heart muscles' fibers which are supplied by that vessel do not receive enough oxygen-rich blood and cannot function properly.

Angina may be brought on by the heart's increased demand for blood above ordinary levels, such as during exercise. Even if

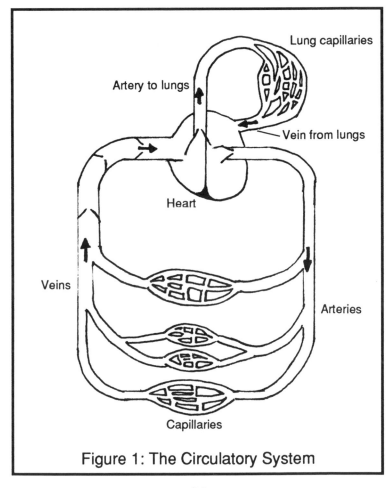

Figure 1: The Circulatory System

the pain is only temporary, it should be considered a warning sign.

If an actual coronary event (heart attack) takes place, the blood supply is cut off from a part of the heart muscle for a period of time. This could be caused by a blood vessel being completely occluded (blocked) by a clot or by plaque, or by a partial occlusion (blockage) complicated by a prolonged spasm.

Depending on the severity of the coronary event, a certain amount of necrosis (cell death) of some heart muscle fiber occurs. After a coronary event, the heart must either recover by replacing dead muscle fibers with scar tissue, or lose its ability to function efficiently. If there is sufficient necrosis, recovery may not be possible.

In considering the steps to reverse heart disease, we must remember that we are not trying to treat mere symptoms. We could get a drug that might thin the blood to the point that hopefully it would not clot and block the blood vessels. We could get a drug that would relax the muscles and perhaps reduce the possibility of spasms. We could do things to lower cholesterol. But such measures do not address the real issue. If we really want to take the necessary steps to reverse heart disease, the first step must be to recognize the underlying problem.

Plaque, the Probable Villain

If plaque is the real villain, we might do well to do a careful character analysis. Let us identify its origin, habitat, and habits.

Its Origin and Habitat

Atherosclerosis occurs only in arteries (blood vessels carrying blood *from* the heart) and not in veins (vessels that carry blood back *to* the heart). Because of this, studying the unique make-up of the arteries will help us see where the plaque begins. While veins are made up of two major layers, arteries are made up of three layers (see Figure 2).

The middle layer of the artery is muscle which allows it to expand and contract with the flow of blood as it is pumped from the heart. This layer also allows the constriction of the blood vessels when the "fight or flight" mechanism is activated by some stress. Such constriction increases blood pressure and forces more nutrients and oxygen into the outermost parts of the body.

It seems that the plaque begins to develop in this muscular

layer. The muscle cells grow in number and proliferate until they begin a buildup on the inner wall of the artery (see Figure 3). When this buildup reaches a certain point, it begins to injure and break the inner lining of the artery.

Its Development and Its Crime

By this time the problem has become much more severe. Material from the bloodstream begins to invade the plaque. The rupture is meanwhile being repaired by fibrin, a protein constituent of the bloodstream, which attempts to seal off the area. However, the net-like texture of fibrin tends to catch other substances that flow by in the bloodstream. This includes materials such as calcium, phospholipids, proteins, triglycerides and cholesterol. It is really only at this point that the often-accused cholesterol enters the picture.

After the cholesterol and calcium have permeated the plaque, it becomes solid and permanent, and atherosclerosis is said to be irreversible. When the heart demands an increased flow of blood, the blood cannot pass this bulge of plaque. Chest pains (angina pectoris) are experienced. A heart attack may not be far away.

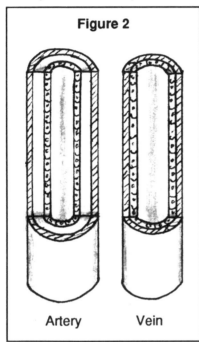

Figure 2

Artery   Vein

So, What is to Blame

While the above analysis gives us a reasonably complete picture, we must still ask, "what really went wrong? Why did the plaque begin and what does it consist of before the calcium and the cholesterol enter the picture?" Probably, there is an instigator behind the scene.

The Free Radical

It seems that the prime suspect in this entire drama may well be a very active group of molecules called "free radicals." These molecules are very unstable, usually of chemical origin and seeking some kind of stability. They are just looking for an opportunity to cause trouble. They cannot rest until they react with something.

Sometimes the free radicals react with the cells of the arterial wall muscles, and sometimes with the lining of the joints. This is why so many treatments useful in cardiac disease are also effective in arthritis.

Now, let us track down the free radical and find out where it comes from, what it does, and how it might be eliminated.

Free radicals are formed in the body by a variety of circumstances which generate these "agents of chemical warfare." The tars in tobacco, rancid unsaturated oils, the inhalation of toxic chemicals, ingestion of chemical additives, and exposure to radiation have all been linked to the formation of free radicals. More specifically, chlorinated water produces chloroform and constipation may produce a powerful free radical called 3-methylcholanthrene.

One of the main activities of the free radical after breaking through the inner wall of the artery is to break into the muscle cells. Once in the cell, the free radical works to confuse the DNA of the cell, thus instigating cell mutation.

Remember that the DNA of the cell is the blueprint for that cell to reproduce itself identically and in proper sequence. If the DNA

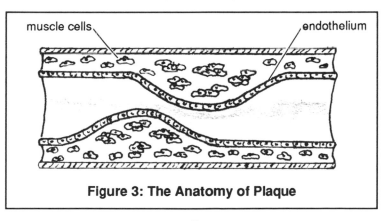

Figure 3: The Anatomy of Plaque

is disturbed or scrambled, the cell no longer has the control factor and may begin to multiply in a distorted or uncontrolled way. This, of course, brings together the necessary factors for a tumor and in the case of the artery, sets the stage for plaque to spawn and prevail.

Obviously then, to strike the root of plaque buildup, we must deal with the free radicals. To do this we need a two-fold approach.

First, we must be willing to pay any price to avoid those factors which generate free radicals and promote their activities.

Second, since the body has a natural immune system to defend itself against the free radicals, we must do all we can to supplement its activity and strengthen its forces.

Later in this chapter, I will develop these two areas.

Early Symptoms

While heart attack, hardening of the arteries and high blood pressure may be obvious signs of circulation problems, many lesser signs may indicate that circulation is weak. If you can answer "yes" to several of the following questions, you should take action to prevent further plaque buildup:

Do your fingers and toes often feel cold?
Do your arms and legs often go to sleep?
Do you have frequent itches?
Do you feel dizzy when you stand up after sitting?
Do you feel a numbness in your limbs?
Does a short walk cause you aches and pains?
Do your legs sting or burn after walking for a while?
Do you get a cramp in your hand when writing?
Is your memory less sharp than it should be?

Records seem to suggest that circulatory problems have reached near-epidemic proportions. When questioned , a mortician indicated that he had not worked on a single cadaver over the age of thirty which did not have some signs of atherosclerosis in the arterial system. In many cases it was hard to pass embalming fluid through the plugged arteries.

Medical Options

While a heart attack is an obvious sign of heart disease, it should be clear by now that the problem does not begin at the moment of attack. According to statistics, medical research, and morticians' observations, a high percentage of our population has some onset of heart disease.

While the object of nutrition is prevention, if heart disease is evident, the following are some current options available.

Nitroglycerin or some other form of nitrates may be used. Some are short-acting and are taken under the tongue when an angina attack comes on; others are long-acting and are taken several times a day.

Nitrates provide relief because they dilate (enlarge) the coronary blood vessels. However, since they dilate the vessels all over the body, headaches, lower blood pressure and occasional fainting may result. Although reasonably effective, they do not correct the fundamental problem.

Propanolol is one of the beta blockers which inhibits certain metabolic functions in order to achieve the desired therapeutic effect. While this may relieve the symptoms, again it does nothing for the fundamental problem and may create problems if one wishes to stop usage.

Cholesterol-lowering drugs are administered with the assumption that cholesterol levels are the real problem. Since it is doubtful that cholesterol is the problem, and since these drugs have little success and many side effects, they are hardly a positive option.

Surgery is yet another alternative chosen by some. As cardiac surgical techniques have improved, more patients are being encouraged to consider surgery. In an open heart operation, the narrowed clogged blood vessels are removed and replaced by grafts of healthy vessels taken from other parts of the body. Although coronary by-pass surgery may somewhat extend life expectancy, it is a serious surgery and does not correct the tendency toward clogged vessels. Given time, atherosclerosis will develop elsewhere, even in the replaced vessels.

Angoplasty is a relatively new technique in which an inflatable balloon is inserted into the artery. When this "balloon" is inflated, it compresses the buildup and stretches the artery. Although angoplasty has some promise for immediate relief, its effect is again only temporary and as a treatment it entirely ignores the reasons why the problem exists.

Chelation Therapy — Intravenous EDTA

The word "chelation" comes from the Greek word "chele" meaning claw, and means to bind. Thus, chelation is the administration of substances which bind certain of the body's minerals, allowing them to be excreted from the body.

In this process a strong chelating synthetic amino acid, ethylene diamine tetra-acetic acid (EDTA), is used. EDTA binds with heavy metals and minerals in the bloodstream. Developed in Germany in the 1930's, chelation became popular in the U.S.A. a decade later as a treatment for lead poisoning as in the case of children who took in lead from paint.

In the case of plaque buildup, the EDTA reduces the mineral content of the bloodstream so that the blood will then pull the calcium from the plaque in order to restore its own balance. The minerals are bound by the EDTA making them unavailable to the body so that they will be eliminated through the kidneys.

The calcium is drawn from the plaque and from the deposits in joints and tendons. Without calcium which acts as a cement, the plaque begins to break up and slowly dissolve being able to once again join the bloodstream.

Each EDTA feeding takes from three to five hours and patients may need twenty to thirty treatments to clean the system. EDTA may be a lifesaver and an attractive alternative to surgery. It must be realized, however, that while it is capable of reversing certain damage to the inner walls of the arteries, it again does not correct the basic cause and should not be considered to be a preventative technique.

The Hope — Oral Chelation

Although heart disease is a complex and controversial subject, recent breakthroughs are shattering the gloomy picture with some bright rays of hope. Oral chelation, a recently developed method of oral artery cleansing, besides bringing debate and controversy, is proving itself to be safe and amazingly effective.

Keith Kenyen, M.D., says, "I sometimes sound extra enthusiastic when I talk about chelation, particularly the oral form. I guess it's because in the twenty-six years I've been practicing medicine, this is the first time I have seen anything as dramatic without side effects."

Kurt Donsbach, Ph.D., speaking of oral chelation, declares, "I have finally seen a phenomenon so exciting, so encouraging, so rewarding, that all other things I have done really become insignificant. I am prepared to stake my reputation that it is now possible to support the circulatory system in a total nutritional way that allows the body to cleanse itself of the offending plaque material which has adhered to the walls of the artery."

Oral chelation is, in the strictest sense, not a chelating action as is the EDTA of intravenous chelation; yet, the end result is the same. The object is two-fold.

1. To strengthen the body's defense system, thus enabling it to destroy and rid itself of free radical activity. This involves strengthening the thymus and other glands as well as keeping the entire body in adequate supply nutritionally.

2. To enable the body to break down plaque, clear up circulatory obstruction and to maintain a constant and adequate supply of oxygen-rich blood to the entire body. This includes nutrients which help to protect us from heavy metals such as lead and arsenic.

Let us consider some of the ingredients necessary for an adequate chelation program and review their functions.

Vitamin A — This essential vitamin is often ranked as one of the most important ones. It increases selenium utilization and guards the mucous membranes against damage. Particularly important in this formula is vitamin A's ability to stimulate the thymus to increase in size, thus triggering more antibody production.

Vitamin C — Important as an antioxidant, vitamin C has many other functions as well. Crucial to this formula is the way in which vitamin C increases our protection against the heavy metals such as lead and arsenic which are able to poison various enzyme reactions in the body. To guard the body against such metals, vitamin C keeps them in solution so that they are discharged with the urine.

Vitamin C also plays an active role in stimulating the production of the enzyme LPL (lipoprotein lipase) which has a "detergent" effect on the arterial wall.

Vitamin E — This indispensable vitamin is a most powerful antioxidant to defend the body from free radicals (for example: superoxides), hydroxyl radicals, peroxides and hydroperoxides.

101

Another outstanding feature found in vitamin E is its function as an amazingly effective antithrombin in the bloodstream. Besides dissolving clots, vitamin E circulating in the blood of a healthy individual will prevent thrombin formation.

Vitamin B-1, B-3 (Niacin), B-5 (Pantothenic Acid), B-6, PABA — As synergistic antioxidants, these vitamins assist the body in inhibiting the formation of damaging free radicals.

A recently published theory put out at Harvard University said that heart disease was caused by a lack of vitamin B-6. Apparently if the body is not sufficiently supplied with this vitamin; methionine, an amino acid which is broken down in the body to cystathionine, cannot properly break down and instead becomes homocysteine, an extremely toxic substance. This theory states that excessive homocysteine actually causes atherosclerosis and that sufficient amounts of vitamin B-6 prevent this toxic metabolite from accumulating.

Choline and Methionine — Choline is a vitamin and methionine an amino acid but both are lipotropics meaning that they aid in the metabolism of fat. Choline also plays a role as part of the neurotransmitter acetylcholine. Methionine works along with many of the detoxification mechanisms in the body.

Selenium — This essential mineral, although actually toxic in several milligram doses, is in microgram doses an absolute necessity for life. When absorbed, it is quickly incorporated into glutathione peroxidase, which is an antioxidant enzyme responsible for the detoxification of hydrogen peroxide and fatty acid peroxides.

We know of vitamin E as a powerful antioxidant but, amazingly, selenium is from 200 to 500 times more potent in this respect than even vitamin E! As antioxidants, selenium and vitamin E work synergistically to inhibit or prevent the damage to tissues caused by free radicals which are considered causal factors in heart disease, atherosclerosis, arthritis and aging.

Zinc — Of great importance in its ability to inhibit free radicals, zinc also promotes the appropriate utilization of vitamin A in the body.

Cysteine Hydrochloride — This amino acid shields the body against the damage of radiation by arresting the free radicals which are produced by ionizing radiation.

An ample supply of cysteine is also essential for the excretion of lead from the tissues. If this lead is not expelled, it may cause irreversible brain damage when accumulated. Thus, cysteine is a most important chelating agent for the elimination of toxic substances.

Thymus Extract — Thymus extract (nucleoprotein) has proven over the years to enhance thymus function which is very crucial in overcoming free radical activity.

Avoiding Killer Number One
What Can I Do?

After identifying the free radicals as the probable instigators behind cell mutation and the formation of plaque, I suggest several steps to attack the problem.

1. Avoid Free Radical Formation

If we take serious steps to avoid the following list of "no-no's," we can be assured that free radical development and its resulting damage will be greatly reduced.

This means, by all means, **avoid:**

1) Smoking — the tars in the tobacco are strongly suspect
2) Consumption of unsaturated oils, particularly rancid oils
3) Exposure to radiation, including x-rays
4) Inhalation of toxic chemicals — This almost requires a mask in today's urban areas.
5) Use of food additives, especially the nitrates, nitrites and other chemical additives
6) Chlorine intake — This is a strong argument for water purification.
7) Constipation — Bowel regularity and occasional colon cleansing is very important (See Chapter 4.).

2. Periodic Body Detoxification

In today's polluted environment, it is impossible to totally avoid all the above-mentioned items, let alone the many other toxic elements around us. While the body can deal with a certain amount of toxins, an overload creates fertile ground for disease to prevail. Because of this, a periodic detoxification program, such as the body cleansing and detoxification program that I outline in chapter four, is a necessity for healthy living in these times.

3. Strengthen the Body's Organic Defenses

The human body was created with an amazing capacity to defend itself against viruses, toxins, and chemical attack including that of free radicals. The prime mechanism for this task is the thymus. The thymus produces lymphocytes which are referred to as "T" cells (an abbreviation for thymus lymphocytes). These "T" cells attack and destroy foreign invaders in the bloodstream and in essence are what we refer to as our immune system. (Chapter five covers the immune system in detail.) Hence, we see that whatever we can do to strengthen our body's defensive immune system, and especially to support the thymus will be a valuable insurance against many diseases.

To strengthen the body's defense system to put a stop to free radical activity and to break down plaque which has already accumulated, I have found the following formula to be effective when followed for two months with an additional month added for every ten years of age over forty:

Vitamin A (34,000 I.U.)	Copper (100 mcg)
Vitamin D (700 I.U.)	Zinc (25 mg)
Vitamin C (2000 mg)	Chromium (135 mcg)
Vitamin B-1 (160 mg)	Selenium (150 mcg)
Vitamin B-2 (50 mg)	Potassium (100 mg)
Vitamin B-6 (140 mg)	Manganese (15 mg)
Vitamin B-12 (75 mcg)	Folic Acid (.30 mg)
Vitamin E (550 I.U.)	Biotin (80 mcg)
Niacin (70 mg)	Choline (380 mg)
Niacinamide (30 mg)	Inositol (50 mg)
Pantothenic Acid (280 mg)	PABA (280 mg)
Calcium (750 mg)	L-Cysteine HCL (750 mg)
Phosphorus (130 mg)	dl-Methionine (180 mg)
Magnesium (400 mg)	Spleen Nucleoprotein (100 mg)
Iron (15 mg)	Adrenal Nucleoprotein (100 mg)
Iodine (150 mcg)	Thymus Nucleoprotein (100 mg)

This of course is a mega-dosage and contains potencies beyond the normal limits. Therefore, it is not to be recommended, advertised or packaged. While any individual may choose to take these amounts, the object of the above is for educational purposes only and should not be construed or promoted as a prescription. Any individual taking or promoting these potencies must bear full responsibility and is advised to consult a qualified health professional.

Of the thousands of people who have followed this program, about five per cent have had the following side effects and offer some suggestions for alleviating these complications.

1. Flatulence — Because of a positive change in the intestinal flora, lower bowel gas may occur for a few days. It will be over within three to seven days.

2. Indigestion — Do not take tablets on an empty stomach but with meals at all times, preferably in a meal containing some protein.

3. Fatigue — Since there may be a considerable release of debris into the bloodstream, a temporary decrease in the ability of the body to carry oxygen may occur. This will produce the need for more rest and relaxation for about seven to ten days. This occurs in the individuals who need assistance the most. It has been found that it is easier for the body to adapt if one begins with a partial dosage and then increases to the full dosage over a period of a few days.

Chapter 10

Sweet Rest — Naturally

While physical, emotional and environmental stress may increase the problem of insomnia, it has been found that if the nutritional balance of the body is proper, sleeping problems may disappear.

When we talk about insomnia, we have to ask *why* our body is keeping us awake. While stress may be a factor, we must inquire further to see why we cannot cope with stress.

In this chapter you will discover:

• Why sleeping pills may actually decrease the amount of quality sleep one gets.

• What foods may be robbing you of the sleep you need.

• How you can actually nourish your body into deeper more restful sleep.

Helps Insomniac

I have been an insomniac most of my adult life. Even if I could fall asleep, I would wake up at the slightest sound and then be awake for hours. There have been periods as long as 3 weeks when I have had no more than three hours sleep a night.

Nine days ago I started following Dr. Zehr's Rest Formula. I have slept for nine nights in a row! I still wake up in the night sometimes, but instead of lying awake for hours getting more and more frustrated and tense, I go back to sleep. Unbelievable!

I.C.

Insomnia

Perhaps the ultimate frustration in life is to exhaust oneself trying to fall asleep. You may be tired. You may need sleep so you can wake up to face another day but sleep just will not come. The condition is called insomnia. Glib advice ranging from counting sheep to thinking in a circle often seems only to complicate matters. Little wonder that every night sleep medications are consumed by millions of "non-sleepers."

Sleep lab investigations have shown that insomniacs need a longer time to enter the first stages of sleep. It has also been found that their deep sleep and rapid eye motion (REM) dream phases are often disturbed. This, as well as tossing and turning, and frequent awakening, makes them feel as though they had no rest at all.

Chemical Complications

Sleeping pills change the sleep patterns, sometimes keeping people from entering REM sleep, and so in fact, may worsen the very problem they are supposed to help. Without REM sleep, a person can not be fully rested.

In addition, sleeping pills may be addictive, causing physical dependency and may disturb normal sleep rhythms. Some induce immediate sleep but do not sustain it over a longer time; others may leave one with a hangover. Each kind has its own set of problems and side effects which the consumer should be fully aware of. One should also be aware that increasingly larger doses may be required to attain the desired effect as the body becomes more tolerant to the medication.

It has also been found that some insomnia problems may be the result of trying to force oneself to get more sleep than the body needs! The better the nutritional intake the less sleep you will probably need.

Caffeine or caffeine-containing drinks (tea, coffee, cola) late in the day may frustrate sleep patterns in some people. Although alcohol may appear to relax and bring sleep, it is a contributor to nighttime hypoglycemia which is a very common cause of nighttime awakening, and when taken with sleeping medications alcohol may be dangerous.

Natural Alternatives

It is exciting and yet relaxing to know that nature has her own tranquilizers. Experiments and experience have shown that there are nutrients that help to induce and maintain sleep. The following nutrients combined in the right amounts have been found to be effective.

L-Tryptophan is the most well-researched nutrient in promoting sleep. It is not a vitamin but an amino acid (one of the building blocks from which proteins are made). It is considered an essential amino acid which means that the body cannot produce it but needs a regular intake. At the Boston State Hospital eleven different studies in the Sleep-Dream laboratory showed tryptophan to be extremely effective and virtually without side effects. In late 1989, suggestions were made that tryptophan might be

-Amino Acids

-RNA

-Lecithin

-Choline

-Inositol

-Herbs

Nutrients to Nourish.

harmful; however, these were not subsequently proven. I would suggest, however, that it is safer and more effective for it to be taken with other factors rather than in isolation.

Niacinamide is a vitamin which enhances the action of tryptophan. For some people it may help to reduce tension and thus have an anti-anxiety effect just by itself. Studies have found niacin effective in relieving mental illness. The amide does not dilate the blood vessels and so will not generate a flush.

Inositol, although considered to be a B vitamin in the United States, is not regarded as a vitamin in Canada. However, according to Robert C. Atkins, M.D., inositol has been proven to be reliable in helping patients to sleep.

Pantothenic Acid, a B vitamin, seems to work well with inositol to enhance relaxation.

Calcium, according to researchers Phillip Goldberg and Daniel Kaufman, may be regarded as the sleep mineral. Calcium levels seem to have an important effect on improving sleep patterns. Hyperactive children can at times be calmed considerably by calcium supplementation. Calcium and magnesium work in proportion to each other most effectively at a two to one ratio.

Magnesium not only conditions the normal activity of the nerves but also stores itself deep in the skeletal muscles to promote the necessary stimuli for muscular control and relaxation and to protect these muscles against spasms.

Alfalfa is the richest land-grown source of trace minerals. It also contains vitamin A and enzymes which assist in digestion. With its numerous other qualities, alfalfa is an excellent base for a nutritional formula.

Chamomile is an excellent general tonic and is promoted widely as a nervine (sedative). It has a gentle soothing effect on the nerves.

Hops is regarded as a powerful, stimulating and relaxing nerve tonic. It increases heart action and capillary circulation, yet will produce soothing slumber in nervous and excited cerebral conditions. Hops also has a relaxing influence upon the liver and gall duct, and is a mild laxative to the bowels.

When using nutritional supplements one should be aware that they work differently from pharmaceutical sleep inducers. Persons who take barbiturates to sleep find that while a small amount seems adequate at the beginning, the dosage needs to be increased as they become habituated to the drugs. With nutrients, on the contrary, a relatively high potency may be taken at the beginning, but the need will gradually diminish as the body's nutritional balance is restored, until eventually no supplementation may be necessary.

Anxiety is somewhat related to insomnia and according to Dr. Atkins those nutrients that are helpful in insomnia are also useful in treating anxiety. For anxiety, however, I would recommend that the supplements should be taken throughout the day in divided doses with meals rather than all at bedtime. The same formula may also be effective in relieving headaches and cramps.

The following herbs in combination have also been found effective for relief from anxiety and restlessness: Valerian, Hops flowers, Passion flower, Chamomile, Wood Betony, Comfrey, Skullcap. Certain individual herbs, such as Chamomile, Wood Betony and Valerian root are traditionally regarded as having a relaxing effect on the human body.

The following forrmula has been found to be a natural and effective aid to better rest:

Natural Sleep and Relaxation Aid
Pantothenic Acid (70 mg)
Niacinamide (35 mg)
Calcium (100 mg)
Magnesium (50 mg)
Inositol (100 mg)
L-Tryptophan (70 mg)
Chamomile (10 mg)
Hops (10 mg)
Alfalfa (10 mg

Chapter 11

Mental Alertness and Nutrition

Today as the general population ages and health deteriorates, we are witnessing an ever-sharpening decline in mental alertness and memory. Despite a steady stream of "how to remember" books, many people are hampered in both their occupational and social lives by the "poor memory plague." Despite new and innovative teaching methods, standardized test scores still slide. To obtain mental alertness and sharp memory, trying harder is not enough, your brain needs food.

In this chapter you will discover:

• How your body's memory works.

• Why your brain needs fuel to stay alert and sharp.

• What nutrients and herbs can work to stimulate production of neurotransmitters.

Increases Mental Alertness

As a student, and not always a diligent one, I often find myself in situations where I have to learn a lot of material in a little time, usually in the wee hours of the morning. You know, the last minute cram. Dr. Zehr's Alertness formula is my life preserver. While my classmates drink coffee that dulls their senses, I feed my brain. Who needs cheat sheets!

R.A.

The Pressure to Remember

The continuing knowledge explosion, and increasingly complicated lifestyles mean more and more things to remember. To cope with this, our memory needs to be sharp, clear and ready for instant recall. The exploding amount of new information that confronts us every day is overwhelming. Consequently, many people begin to feel inadequate. "I keep forgetting;" "I can't remember what I just read," and "I forgot to call back," are just some of the common frustrations. While we cannot add new computer "disks" to our brain, we can do a lot to sharpen and activate what we do have. The results of scientific findings bring new hope and brighter futures to virtually all of us.

The Chemistry of Remembering

Recent findings have shown that we can purposely stimulate the brain's production of neurotransmitters by taking specific nutrients in supplement form. Neurotransmitters are chemicals which relay messages between neurons. When this relay process is facilitated, mental alertness and memory recall are increased.

In recent years tremendous advances have been made in our understanding of the biochemical mechanisms basic to thought and intelligence. Since the body is like a big chemical plant, it can take raw materials apart and put them back together in a form acceptable to meet its needs. All that is needed are the right ingredients in the right combinations and our body can work wonders. It can even meet the demands of today's stressful lifestyle. Supplementation, then, is an added supply of the required ingredients to help the body help itself.

117

Activating Natural Alertness

The discovery of the amazing effects of nutrients other than vitamins and minerals is just beginning to open new ways to help our bodies help themselves. The following nutrients are all involved in facilitating the mental processes. Putting them together should be a very significant step toward bringing many persons up to top alertness! Most often it is not that we do not have what it takes, but rather that what we do have cannot function at its peak level because it is short on the needed supply. The factors listed below are some of the "brain fuel" ingredients necessary for top performance.

Phenylalanine is an essential amino acid which appears to play an important role in learning and memory. It is used by the brain to manufacture norepinephrine which brain nerve cells use to stimulate each other. When norepinephrine is depleted, depression and difficulties in learning and memory may occur.

L Glutamine is a unique substance in that it is one of the few nutrients in addition to glucose that can be used as fuel by the brain cells. Glutamic acid itself does not pass through the "blood brain barrier," only in the glutamine form will it cross the barrier. Test groups of mentally retarded children taking glutamine have shown favorable results. Because of these tests, some physicians now prescribe glutamine for mentally deficient patients.

"Sumtimz stayin awake jest aint a nuff."

Stu Dent

Even when only moderate amounts of glutamine are taken, there is a marked elevation of glutamic acid in the brain.

RNA (Ribonucleic Acid) is an important natural substance for learning and memory. It has been shown to improve intellectual performance in animals. Current scientific evidence supports the idea that learning and the ability to retain new memories involve the creation of RNA on which actual information is coded.

Lecithin — Choline — Inositol. Lecithin which already contains choline and inositol can be fortified with even higher concentrations of these two substances, both of which are essential to brain function. Acetylcholine is a neurotransmitter, a substance which many nerve cells in certain parts of the body use to stimulate each other. Its concentration in the brain cells declines sharply with age.

Gotu Kola, Ginseng, Eyebright and Kelp are herbs which are time-proven aids to human health, created to meet all of mankind's needs. These herbs in proper combination can complement the above factors to invigorate memory and brain function.

Gotu kola is universally acknowledged to contain rejuvenating properties able to strengthen the heart, the memory and the brain. Tradition states that this valuable herb increases the oxygen level to the brain. Therefore, it has been much used as an aid in alleviating conditions related to nutritional deficiencies of the brain and memory functions.

Ginseng is highly lauded in the Far East for slowing down the aging process and it has been established that both physical and mental efficiency are improved by its use. It has been stated that a combination of Gotu Kola and Ginseng stimulates mental and physical work ability, relieves signs of brain fatigue and improves mental and physical reflex action. In addition, it aids in acceleration and acquisition of learning, and improves the work of the brain cells.

Eyebright, long recognized as having a beneficial effect on eyesight, also has a strong and positive effect on the forehead region, clearing not only physical but also mental vision.

Being rich in many minerals, especially iodine, kelp provides the necessary minerals which facilitate the function of all the other ingredients in this combination.

In addition to the above nutrients, other vitamins and minerals are, of course, also involved in proper mental function. Some which play an important role are as follows:

1. Vitamin C is concentrated in various parts of the brain and in the pituitary gland. Studies show that the brain is more sensitive to vitamin C deficiency than are other organs such as the liver.

2. Vitamin B-12 is an active coenzyme influencing the brain and especially the nerves. Among the symptoms of B-12 deficiency are memory disturbance, learning impairment and mental confusion.

3. Folic Acid is essential to the functioning of the brain, being selectively concentrated in the spinal fluid and extracellular fluid.

4. Potassium is responsible for transmitting electrical impulses and is highly active in the nervous system.

5. B-15's amazing capacity to enable the blood to contain and carry more oxygen is also a vital factor in mental alertness.

Memory and Mental Alertness Formula

From the above knowledge and information, I would suggest a special supplement to assure maximum memory and brain efficiency.

Phenylalanine (100 mg)   Kelp (100 mg)
L-Glutamine (100 mg)   Lecithin (500 mg)
Ribonucleic Acid (100 mg)   PABA (50 mg)
Ginseng (100 mg)   Choline (30 mg)
Gotu Kola (100 mg)   Inositol (15 mg)
Eyebright (100 mg)

Chapter 12

Traditional Uses of Selected Herbs

Since prehistoric times, man has appreciated the wonderful healing properties of herbs. Yet, as science has become better able to analyze and synthesize, we have left our medicinal roots and sought to replace them with laboratory products. As medical "breakthroughs" are heralded, herbs are ridiculed and good health in its truest sense is slipping into extinction. Perhaps it is time to come back to our roots.

In this chapter you will discover:

• What is the significance of herbs in the human diet.

• What is the history of the medicinal usage of various herbs.

• What herbs have been taditionally used for various diseases and health problems. Diseases highlighted in italics.

The human body was created to be sustained by air, water and food. The primary source of human food is intended to be plants. The same Creator who created man also created plants with the intention that they should meet all the needs of man including his medicinal needs. For our purposes, we would categorize plants into three categories :

1. Basic Food — this would include plants which supply the basic nutritional needs of man, and could be consumed on a regular basis. This would include the common vegetables and fruits.

2. Supplementary — this would include plants which have been found to contain an unusually high amount of certain nutrients. They might be considered to help to alleviate a specific deficiency. An early example of this category would be the case of sailors eating lemons or limes to overcome scurvey which we now know to be the result of a vitamin C deficiency. Another example might be taking prunes to help in regularity.

3. Medicinal — in this category, we would put those plants, primarily herbs, which have proven through history to have distinct curative or medicinal effects on the body. Historically these have not been regarded as daily food, but have been taken periodically or for specific maladies because they contained mysterious factors which brought about healing. In some cases, science has isolated these factors and now uses them in synthetic forms for some modern medicines.

In the following pages we will list some of the most common herbs that might be considered to be in the third category, and give some of their historically accepted uses. A handy herb reference guide can be found in Appendix B.

Alfalfa

It was with great respect that the ancient Arabs crowned alfalfa "the Father of all Foods." Alfalfa has a history of dramatic usefulness to the human race.

This plant has been known to send its feeder roots as far as fifty feet into the earth, seeking out valuable minerals. It is no surprise, then, that alfalfa is the richest land-grown source of trace minerals. It also contains eight digestive enzymes, protein and calcium along with other minerals. Alfalfa is rich in vitamin content as well and is most famous for containing vitamins U and P (rutin).

Digestive disorders seem to benefit from alfalfa. Noting the vitamin U content in alfalfa, it is clear why this herb is especially good for *peptic ulcers.*

Kidney and bladder troubles also respond well to alfalfa as it makes excretion of the kidneys less acidic and therefore less irritating to the urinary tract.

Steady doses of alfalfa spread throughout the day often bring tremendous relief to *arthritis* sufferers.

Including alfalfa in one's diet can serve as an excellent health tonic and assure adequate mineral intake.

Barley Green

Barley green is a nutrient-rich powder from the tender young barley plant. The rich green juice is spray dried and blended with the barley fiber in order to preserve the full value of the amazing contents found in the young barley plant.

After researching 150 different green plants, herbs, and grasses, Dr. Yoshihide Hagiwara, M.D., a noted Japanese pharmacologist, concluded that the best source of nutrition was the rich young barley leaf. Howard Lutz, Director for the Institute of Preventative Medicine in Washington, D.C. says that barley green is one of the most incredible products of this decade.

Barley green contains chlorophyll, live enzymes, alkalinity p.h., amino acids, 16 vitamins and 23 minerals.

Chlorophyll is the main ingredient in barley green and gives it its green color. It has a healing, cleansing and detoxifying effect on the human body. As chlorophyll *cleanses the intestinal tract*, it leaves behind its rich food elements. Chlorophyll also works to *clean, heal and restore the liver.* It *removes poisons that collect in the blood, tissues and glands* such as lead from automobile exhaust and mercury in drinking water. Laboratory investigations indicate that cell activity and its normal regrowth are increased by the use of chlorophyll. It is absorbed directly through the cell membranes of the mouth, stomach and intestines.

More than 20 enzymes are present in barley green. Science has determined that all chemical changes in our cells are performed by enzymatic actions. Enzymes functioning with minerals perform and promote synthesis and decomposition under normal conditions. Enzymes function to digest food and oxygen entering the bloodstream, thus creating new cells. Some weight gain is caused by the inability of enzymes to decompose fats within the body. Although the body makes its own enzymes, poor chewing, weak digestion and processed foods make this difficult. The available enzymes in barley green help this process.

By relying on processed foods, North Americans have caused a high acid imbalance in their bodies. Some experts believe that acid diet and disease are related. The alkaline factor like that in barley green works to restore the proper p.h. balance and thus creates a better environment for good health.

Barley green contains 18 amino acids including the eight essential ones. Amino acids are necessary for the growth and maintenance of the body and are commonly referred to as the building blocks of life.

Barley green has helped people with a wide range of afflictions, from *acne, allergies* and *arthritis* to *diabetes, digestion* and *depression*, as well as *kidneys, cramps* and *high blood pressure.* Being a very mild and totally natural food, barley green is entirely safe to be taken in any amount.

Bee Pollen

Health scientists have called it "the only super-perfect food on earth." Amazingly, bee pollen contains every basic element found in the human body which must be renewed by nutrient intake.

Bee pollen contains a remarkable 35% protein about half of which is found as free amino acids. Even a weak digestive system can handle free amino acids because they are immediately assimilated by the body for rebuilding and rejuvenating. Rutin, aspartic acid and many enzymes (such as phosphatase, amylase and diastase), as well as all the known vitamins are present in bee pollen.

Many athletes swear by bee pollen as a safe aid to *body building* without producing increased fat.

Pernicious anemia and disturbances of the intestinal system such as *colitis* and *chronic constipation* have responded well to bee pollen.

Carlson Wade, author of *Bee Pollen and Your Health,* praises bee pollen, "The healing, rejuvenating and disease-fighting effects of this total nutrient are hard to believe, yet are fully documented. *Aging, digestive upsets, prostate disease, sore throats, acne, fatigue, sexual problems, allergies,* and a host of other conditions have been successfully treated by the use of bee pollen."

Black Cohosh

With the North American Indians Black Cohosh has long held a place of respect. Their women especially have used it for a wide range of female complaints.

This herb is most famous for its content of natural estrogen. It also contains significant amounts of calcium, potassium and magnesium.

Black Cohosh has a history of usefulness in a wide variety of female problems such as *hot flashes*, and *menstrual pain* . It is said to have a calming effect during and after *childbirth*.

This herb has also proven useful in cases of *high blood pressure, rheumatism, arthritis* and *neuralgia.* It *loosens and expels mucus from the bronchial tubes* while stimulating the secretions of the *liver, kidneys* and *lymphs.*

It is a *heart tonic,* equalizing blood circulation and neutralizing poisons in the bloodstream while expelling uric acid and toxic wastes.

Black Walnut Leaves

For many people the name Black Walnut means welcome relief from dreaded *parasites* and *worms.* But there are additional qualities to note in this herb.

Black Walnut leaves' high percentage of an organic iodine (potassium iodine) is responsible for this herb's amazing ability to kill animal or vegetable parasites within the body and to expel worms from the system.

Being rich in vitamin B-15, Black Walnut oxygenates the *blood* and is useful for *varicose veins.* It helps to balance *sugar levels,* and burn up excess toxins and fatty materials in the system. The rich manganese content makes Black Walnut excellent for *bilious and intestinal cramping.*

Capsicum

Capsicum (also called cayenne) holds title as the single most useful herb. This is due to the fact that for any kind of body healing to take place, stimulation is the key. Capsicum is prized as the purest and best *stimulant* known in the entire plant kingdom.

Capsicum is rich in vitamin A, C, iron, calcium and potassium. Acting as a catalyst, capsicum will *increase the power of all other herbs,* sending them quickly to the parts of the body where they are needed, and there enhance their effectiveness.

In cases of a *flu* or *cold, diarrhea* or *dysentery with blood,* capsicum is very helpful. This herb has also been used successfully to aid in *digestion.* It will even rebuild the tissue on the *stomach* and heal stomach and intestinal *ulcers.* It is also used for the *heart* and *kidneys* as well as for *rheumatism* and *varicose veins.*

Cascara Sagrada

When the early Spanish priests discovered the exciting medicinal qualities of this tree bark used by the Indians, they named it "Cascara Sagrada," meaning the sacred bark.

Cascara contains B Complex, calcium, potassium and manganese and is rich in hormone-like oils which produce peristaltic action in the *intestinal canal.*

Cascara has an excellent reputation in cases of habitual and chronic *constipation.* It is useful in cases of *hemorrhoids* or *piles.* Cascara is one of the safest natural laxatives ever discovered and is not habit forming. Also beneficial to the gall ducts, cascara sagrada will help the body rid itself of *gall stones.*

Chamomile

Since ancient times chamomile's gentle action has made it a favorite for *children's ailments.* Many doctors in France and Spain still prescribe this herb for various childhood illnesses. But adults too have much to gain from chamomile.

Chamomile is rich in calcium and magnesium.

This herb is a relaxant, soothing to the nerves with no side effects. For babies with *upset stomachs* and *colic,* it is one of the best herbs for soothing and *inducing sleep.* In women chamomile will relieve *congestion in the uterus,* stimulate the *menstrual flow* and remedy *nervous conditions during the menstrual period.*

Chamomile is said to have helped people through the difficulties of *drug withdrawal.* It is often used for *fevers* and *bronchitis.*

Chaparral

As so many people have claimed that this humble desert plant produces an *anti-cancer action,* researchers have given it much attention and found some exciting results.

Chaparral contains the active ingredient nordihydroguairetic acid (NDGA) which has the ability to convert imbalanced fermentation processes. Chaparral functions as a strong antioxidant, destroying harmful bacteria.

An excellent *blood purifier* and *liver cleanser,* chaparral is also a powerful healer to the *urethral tract* and to the *lymphatics.*

Chaparral is known as an *anti-tumor agent* and holds a reputation of usefulness in cases of *acne* and *arthritis.*

Chickweed

Chickweed has established a solid reputation as a dieter's best friend. This well-known *appetite depressant* contains potassium which seems to satisfy the craving for food.

Chickweed is also rich in iron, calcium, Vitamins C and B Complex.

Chickweed is effective for *lung complaints.* It will soothe and heal all forms of *inflamation of the membranes,* both internal and external. This herb activates the body's *burning of fat,* removes *fatty tumors* and *mucus in the throat.*

Comfrey

As early as 400 B.C. the Greeks were using comfrey to *stop bleeding* and to heal *bronchial troubles.*

The English word "comfrey" comes from the Latin "confervere" which means "to join together." People discovered, to their amazement, that when comfrey was cooked together with meat, it caused the pieces to join together. This observation led them to the happy discovery that comfrey could close up *wounds* and help to knit *broken bones.*

We now know that comfrey contains a special healing agent, allantoin. This allantoin promotes cell growth and speeds up the healing of wounds, internal irritations and broken bones.

Comfrey is also greatly valued in treating *respiratory ailments* as it soothes and heals inflamed tissues, aids the bronchial tubes by increasing *expectoration* and serves as a general stimulant to the *mucous membrane.*

The allantoin and mucilaginous agents in comfrey make it particularly healing to *inflamed or ulcerated tissue in the gastrointestinal tract.*

Damiana

Dr. M.H. Myers (M.D.) of Philadelphia gives strong support for the use of damiana, "I have given it quite an extensive trial in my practice, and as a result I find that in cases of partial or other *sexual debility,* its success is universal. I pronounce it the most effective and only remedy that in my hands had a successful result in all cases."

Damiana is known to be an effective *sexual rejuvenator* in lethargy of the sexual organs. It is also highly regarded as a cure for *female complaints* due to *female hormone imbalance.*

Damiana's effectiveness, though great, may not be noticed immediately.

Dandelion Root

As early as the tenth century Arabian physicians were using the dandelion as medicine. The dandelion root has an amazingly high vitamin and mineral content. For example, it contains 7,000 units of Vitamin A per ounce, the highest of all plants.

The root also contains a number of various sugar compounds which are necessary for energy and strength. One of these, inulin, has been called "diabetic sugar" and has sometimes been used *instead of insulin.* This inulin also stimulates the secretion of the *pancreas* and *spleen* and increases the overall activity of the *liver* which is important for cleansing the body. The liver is also benefited by the choline (a B vitamin) and the valuable alkaloid, taraxacin found in dandelion, especially in cases of *hepatitis* or *inflammation of the liver* and *jaundice.*

Dandelion is an excellent purifying agent for it contains all the nutritive salts necessary for the body to *purify the blood.*

Many cultural groups have claimed the dandelion to be wonderful in treating *skin diseases, eczema* and *psoriasis.*

Echinacea

Back in 1885 echinacea was introduced into American medicine by Dr. H.C.F. Meyer as a *blood purifier.* But by now, we know that this one herb alone contains a gold mine of medicinal properties.

Swiss research has found this plant to contain these exciting ingredients: *antibiotic* glycosides; *immune-stimulating* polysaccharides; a variety of *bacteriostatic and fungastatic* polyacetylenes; a polyene with *anti-tumor* activity; echinacein, a complex amide with *insecticidal and antiviral* activity; and an unknown substance with a cortisone-like activity against *inflammation* which also stimulates the cells active in *tissue regeneration* and *elimination of infectious organisms.*

Richard J. Dolman shares his excitement in discovering that this "plant extract could be more important to North American pharmaceutical therapy than penicillin. . . . exactly what North American adherents to alternative medicine have been looking for to offset the tide of synthetic drugs: a genuinely effective natural antibiotic."

This plant has the ability to stimulate the immune system. It also *purifies the blood, stregthens the prostate* and possesses *anti-inflammatory and anti-allergy properties.*

Another amazing factor which only the Creator of nature could implement is the fact that there exists a special relationship between echinacea and the biochemistry of the human body.

Eyebright

The eyesight of those who ate this plant began to show remarkable improvement and thus it was that the word chosen to represent this plant in the English language is "Eyebright."

Eyebright is extremely rich in vitamins A and C. It has antiseptic qualities that make it useful in *eye infections.* Its cooling and detoxifying properties make eyebright effective in cases of *inflammation.*

Eyebright has the ability to *strengthen all of the eye tissues.* The nerve and optic devices responsible for vision become much more elastic and resilient with regular use of this herb. On the other hand, if any of these parts are too lax, eyebright will tighten them up to a healthy condition. Thus, according to John Heinerman, medical herb specialist and medical anthropologist, "the chemical constituents of eyebright regulate the tensile strength of all fibrous mass in the eyes, by either tightening them up or relaxing them as the case may be."

Eyebright has also been used for *allergies, hayfever, mumps, measles and chickenpox.* But this herb is most famous for its use in eye ailments such as *eye inflammation, conjunctivitis, ulcers, failing vision* and *eye strain.*

Garlic

Garlic is undoubtedly nature's wonder food, packed full of many health-giving properties. Yet sadly, its intense odor and subsequent social implications have turned away many would-be garlic users. Now however, with the availability of odorless garlic in capsule form, there is nothing to stop the general population from enjoying all the healthful effects of garlic.

Garlic has established quite a reputation as *"nature's antibiotic"* due to the active substance, allicin, found in garlic. Garlic does not destroy the body's normal flora as many antibiotics tend to do.

Garlic is a popular remedy for those who are susceptible to *colds, chronic fatigue* and *general sluggishness.* Even people in general good health can benefit from this disease-preventative herb as it *builds resistance, increases vigor* even in extreme temperature conditions, and speeds up recovery time should one become sick.

Garlic is excellent for *lowering blood pressure.* In using garlic for patients with *hypertension,* Dr. F.G. Piotrowski found that it not only reduced the blood pressure but also was effective against the symptoms of *dizziness, angina-like pain, headaches* and *backaches* after three to five days of treatment.

In improving *digestion,* garlic is helpful as it stimulates the gastric juices and arrests intestinal putrefacation and infection while increasing the presence of friendly bacteria.

The allicin and sulphur-related compounds found in garlic make it effective against *parasites* and *worms* in the body.

Ear infections respond well to garlic. A simple way to treat the infection is to puncture a garlic capsule and squeeze the garlic oil into the ear.

Ginger

Most people limit ginger's role to that of a flavoring agent in such favorites as gingerbread and ginger ale or as a standard component in Oriental cuisine. In actuality ginger is a real marvel in the world of natural remedies.

Ginger works very well in combination with other herbs as it will increase their effectiveness. Ginger is excellent for signs of indigestion such as *upset stomach* or *intestinal gas.* It is a reliable remedy in fighting a *cold* or *flu.* It will eliminate *congestion* and *headaches* and ease the pain of *sore throats.* It is a valuable tonic for the respiratory system in general and works especially well with capsicum to clear *bronchial congestion* or a *stuffy nose.*

Ginger works far better than leading drugstore varieties of motion sickness preventatives to combat the dreaded *car sickness* and other forms of *motion sickness.* Ginger's success was confirmed by a recent study at Utah's Brigham Young University. Dr. Dennis Clayson, co-author of the study said that, "Taking 2 capsules of ginger can stop motion sickness in its tracks." He recommended taking the ginger 15 minutes before boarding a plane, boat or car. Some people may find two capsules to be sufficient for an entire trip while others may require two or even up to four or five capsules each hour. "You can't overdose," notes Dr. Daniel Mowrey, co-author of the study, "If you begin to take more than you need, you'll have a mild burning sensation in the upper chest-throat area. Quit taking them when you reach that point."

Ginseng

In Ezekiel 27:17 we discover that ginseng (then called Pannag) was already being traded in the marketplace of Israel. Respected for centuries in China, this healing root is considered a cure-all by the Chinese.

This herb will stimulate both *physical and mental vigor* when taken initially but its effect is even more noticeable when taken for a period of six months or more.

Ginseng seems to *slow down the aging process* as it supplies important hormones and also increases resistance to physical, chemical and biological types of *stress.* Physical stress would include exposure to *radiation, temperature extremes* and excessive physical activity. Chemical stress refers to the body's encounter with *drugs, poisons or toxic chemicals. Bacteria and tumors* are examples of biological stress.

Golden Seal

Golden seal is one of the best general medicinal herbs in the plant kingdom. It is invaluable taken both alone and with other herbs to increase their tonic properties.

The two principle constituents of golden seal, hydrastine and berberine explain its *antibiotic* and *antiseptic* qualities. Golden seal is a *natural source of insulin.* All the *mucous membranes* (including those lining the stomach, sinuses, small intestine, colon, lungs, kidneys and bladder) benefit from golden seal's healing power. This herb is effective in any *catarrhal condition* whether it be in the nasal area, throat, bronchial tubes, stomach, intestines or bladder. Golden seal will also help to regulate the *liver function* and arrest *internal bleeding.*

Gotu Kola

Gotu kola is well-deserving of its reputation as "the brain food." An important constituent found in this herb is asiaticoside (a triterpene glycoside) which exerts a stimulating energy on the central nervous system. This in turn activates the functioning of the brain.

Gotu kola is excellent for *mental fatigue, senility,* and improving the *memory* capacity. It will also increase the *physical energy* level.

Gotu kola is valuable in rebuilding energy reserves after a *nervous breakdown* and may prevent such a condition in the first place.

Hawthorne Berry

Hawthorne berry is a wonderful heart tonic. The berries contain vitamins B17, C and A, pectin, hydrocyanic acid and other constituents which will prevent or reduce *atherosclerosis* in the heart valves. These ingredients are also responsible for hawthorne berries' incredible ability to decrease weight in serious cases of *obesity.* They exert a catabolic effect on fatty adipose tissue, meaning that they "burn up" fat.

Especially when taken together with capsicum, hawthorne berry is excellent for lowering *blood pressure.*

Taken regularly, hawthorne berry will strengthen the *heart muscles.* It has proven effective in so many heart ailments including *irregular heart rhythm, heart valve defects, enlarged heart, angina pectoris, mitral stenosis,* and *heart disease of old age.*

Horsetail (Shavegrass)

In the Middle Ages the horsetail plant was commonly found in the kitchen — but not for eating. It was the dishwasher's best friend, prized for its scouring power when used on pewter-ware, wooden kitchen utensils and milkpails. Then someone started eating the plant and the results were exciting.

Horsetail contains a very high percentage of silicon, an essential trace mineral. Silicon is found in our body's connective tissues such as cartilage, tendons, and blood vessels and is necessary to keep these tissues resilient and strong.

The silicon content of horsetail seems also to be responsible for its great benefits to the *finger and toe nails, hair, teeth* and *bones.*

Horsetail holds a reputation as a healer in cases of *kidney and dropsical disorders, skin and eye problems, internal bleeding, urinary and menstrual disorders,* and for strengthening the *heart* and the *lungs.*

Kelp

Kelp is a real treasure from the sea. This seaweed actually contains more vitamins and minerals than any other single food. It contains nearly 30 minerals, including some very important trace minerals.

The iodine found in kelp will stimulate the *thyroid* and thus increase the body's *metabolism* thus aiding in *weight reduction.* Kelp contains alginic acid and other micronutrients which help to cleanse the *arteries* by absorbing the toxic substances. Kelp is a good tonic for *hormonal balance* particularly for the *prostate.*

Licorice Root

Licorice Root has a rich vitamin content which includes

important vitamins such as vitamin E, B-complex, niacin and pantothenic acid.

This herb holds a good reputation for its usefulness in helping *coughs, colds and sore throats.* It is healing to any *inflammation of the intestinal tract* and also to *duodenal, peptic and gastric ulcers.* Licorice root will stimulate the *adrenal glands* and help to counteract *stress.* Licorice root is also valued for its effectiveness in cases of *impotency, female complaints* (exerting a natural estrogenic activity), *hypoglycemia* and *constipation.*

Lobelia

Often nicknamed "Indian Tobacco" because of its taste, this herb is in no way related to the tobacco plant. Rather, it was collected by the North American Indians in late summer and early fall to stock their medicine reserves for the winter months.

Lobelia was much prized as an important aid in *respiratory ailments* including *asthma, bronchial spasms, pneumonia* and *coughing.*

Lobelia also holds claim as the most powerful *relaxant* in the plant kingdom, soothing the entire *nervous system.* Because of its diffusable nature, lobelia is best used along with other herbs such as capsicum, a permanent stimulant.

Mullein

For centuries mullein has held an important place in medicine around the world. In the Middle Ages it was popularized in Russia. For several hundred years the North American Indians have successfully used it for *hemorrhoids* taking it both internally and as a fomentation.

The Indians were also known to smoke the dried mullein leaves to alleviate *lung congestion.* Today we acknowledge mullein as a valuable healer in *respiratory and pulmonary complaints.* It is recommended for *coughs, colds, hoarseness, shortness of breath* and *bronchitis.* It will loosen and expel *mucus* from the body.

Mullein is a natural *painkiller,* yet it will not become habit forming. It relaxes the nerves and will calm *cramps* or *spasms.* Problems of the *digestive tract* also respond favorably to the use of mullein, and it is especially useful in cases of *colitis.*

Poke Root

Herbalists consider poke root to be one of the most powerful alteratives in the plant kingdom. It tones the system, stimulates *metabolism* and *cleanses the blood* while it helps to expel waste from the body. This makes it useful in treating *obesity.*

This herb is recommended for *rheumatism, arthritis* and any type of *inflammation.* It will support the *glandular system,* especially in problems of the *thyroid* and *spleen.* Poke root is also useful in relieving *liver or kidney congestion.*

Safflower

Safflower is a useful herb to keep on hand for childhood ailments. It is reliable in cases of *eruptive diseases, colds* and *viral infections.* It will arrest a *fever* by promoting perspiration.

Safflower has gained popularity among *hypoglycemics* who claim it relieves fatigue and muscle cramps after physical exertion or exercise. It is also recommended for *jaundice, sluggish liver* and *gallbladder ailments.*

Sarsaparilla

The North American Indians used sarsaparilla extensively, eating the root as their staple food on long hunting expeditions. This is not surprising when we discover that Sarsaparilla has a rich vitamin and mineral content and is high in oxygen. It also contains valuable hormones which are excellent in cases of m*ale or female hormone imbalances.* When combined with ginseng, sarsaparilla has been effective in helping teenage boys with *complexion problems* due to hormone imbalances.

Back in the mid-1800's sarsaparilla gained nationwide popularity in the United States as a tonic for "spring-cleaning" the body. It was used to flush out poisons from the blood and to cleanse the system from any lingering signs of winter ailments. It is now recognized as an excellent *blood purifier* and an effective *antidote for poisons.*

Sarsaparilla will *expel gas* from the stomach and intestines. It is also used for *rheumatism, ringworm, gout* and *skin disorders,* including *psoriasis.*

Spirulina

Spirulina is a simple one-celled form of algae. These microorganisms might be called the most basic "food factories" because they rely on the power of the sun to create life-giving nutrients through photosynthesis. Because algae occupy the bottom position on the food chain, they meet some of the most basic food needs of every cell of higher organisms. Even great whales live and exist on algae.

Among the various forms of algae, spirulina has been found to be the richest and most food efficient. Spirulina is 65 to 71 per cent complete protein, with all of the essential amino acids in perfect balance; beef is only 22 per cent protein. In addition, its photosynthetic process is almost three times more efficient than that of land-growing plants such as soybeans.

Spirulina also provides high concentrations of amino acids, chelated minerals, trace elements and enzymes. It is one of the few plant sources of vitamin B-12, usually found in animal tissues.

Spirulina has been used by medical establishments both in Mexico and Japan. Experiments in Japan have demonstrated that spirulina has a very positive effect on *anemia, liver disease,* and *allergies.* It has also brought about noticeable improvements in the condition of *diabetics* as well as increasing their *overall vigor* and *sense of well being. Ulcers* and *visual complaints* were also cleared up. Studies have shown that spirulina can slow the loss of white blood cells due to *chemotherapy* and *radiation,* and can forestall *pancreatic exhaustion.* In cases of *heavy metal contamination,* the excretion of cadmium, lead and mercury was stimulated by spirulina in test patients.

Thyme

Thyme contains vitamins C, D and B complex. These ingredients undoubtedly explain its usefulness in *nervous disorders.* It will quickly exert a soothing sedative effect on the nerves and in cases of *hysteria* or *headache.*

Thyme is also useful in cases of *asthma, whooping cough, colic, suppressed menstruation, irritable stomach* and *gas,* and will soothe the *throat* in cases of *bronchial irritation.*

Uva Ursi

Uva ursi (also known as bearberry) holds a remarkable reputation as a healer to the *urinary organs* as it will strengthen and tone the mucous membranes of the urinary passages. The arbutin content in uva ursi acts as a valuable antiseptic in killing *viral infection* in the urinary organs. Uva ursi also contains allantoin which explains its ability to relieve the pain of *kidney inflammation.* In conditions of gravel or ulceration of the kidneys or *bladder,* uva ursi has proven helpful as well. Even in old cases of *gonorrhea, leucorrhoea and chronic urethritis,* sufferers have found relief with uva ursi.

Uva ursi is of great value in *diabetes.* It is also used for cases of excessive *menstruation* and other *female complaints.*

Valerian Root

Valerian root is best known for its safe sedative effect on the nervous system. It is used in cases of *nervous disorders, muscle twitching, spasms, hysteria, nervous headache, restlessness, epileptic fits, pain* and to prevent *sleeplessness.*

White Willow Bark

Tablets and papyri from the ancient Sumerians and Egyptians prescribe white willow bark for a wide variety of ailments. Hippocrates, the father of modern medicine was well aware of its healing powers and prescribed it frequently for pain and fever.

About the turn of the century, scientists suceeded in isolating the principal active ingredient in the bark, salicin. They further determined that the body converts this salicin into salicylic acid. "Why not," they reasoned, "simply make salicylic acid synthetically?" They began to commercially manufacture the substance which soon became known as aspirin and since it was easy to make, it soon replaced white willow bark.

White willow bark, of course, has none of the side effects that aspirin has. This is no doubt due largely to the presence of other organic compounds which aspirin does not contain.

The many uses of white willow bark could be categorized into three groups: as a *fever-lowering* agent, probably facilitating the dissipation of heat through increased peripheral blood flow and sweating; as a *pain-relieving* agent; and as an *anti-inflammatory* agent for the treatment of *rheumatism* and *arthritis*.

It has also been reported to be effective when used for *headaches, debility of digestive organs, dandruff, eye problems, malaria, chills, influenza, eczema* and *nosebleed*.

White Oak Bark

White oak bark is useful both internally or externally (as an enema or douche) for *menstrual difficulties, blood in the urine, rectal problems* and in cases of *hemorrhoids* it can be taken internally and applied topically (acute cases would require a fairly high dosage). *Varicose veins* respond well to white oak bark when it is used internally and externally at the same time.

White oak bark has a history of usefulness in *chronic diarrhea, chronic mucus discharges, internal hemorrhage, bleeding cuts*, and *inflammation*. Used as a tea it makes a good gargle for *sore throats*.

Wood Betony

Wood betony is best known for its success in treating *head and face pains*. Its sedative effect makes it useful for treating *headaches, nervousness and hysteria*. It is often used for a children's sedative.

Heartburn, indigestion and *stomach cramps* respond very well to wood betony. It has also been used successfully in cases of *Parkinson's disease, jaundice, worms,* and congestion of the *liver* and *spleen*.

Yellow Dock

Yellow Dock holds a strong reputation as a *blood purifier*. As it purifies the blood, it cleanses *boils* and *ulcers*. It has been successful in dissolving *tumors*. *Ulcerated eyelids, running discharge of the ears,* and *skin disorders including eczema, psoriasis, cradlecap, hives, acne and itching* respond well to yellow dock.

Yellow Dock is rich in organic iron as well as vitamins A and C. The iron content makes it one of the most outstanding *blood builders* in the natural world and also useful for *female weakness due to iron deficiency* and *liver problems*.

Yucca

The yucca root is very rich in vitamins A and B complex and has a high mineral content, calcium and potassium being especially worthy of note. It also contains a high content of steroid saponins which explains its excellent reputation in cases of *arthritis* and *rheumatism,* especially when the yucca is taken along with chaparral.

Yucca is an effective *blood purifier,* making it valuable in *skin disorders* as well.

Chapter 13

Herbal Combinations for Greater Kick

While every health disorder can be identified by a set of basic similarities, when found in different people there may be some unique aspects relative to that person's personal history and unique body chemistry. To confront these differences, herbalists sometimes use combinations of herbs.

Just as every human being has a unique fingerprint, so everyone has a unique body chemistry. This factor is referred to as a biochemical individuality. Each one of us is the composite total of our birth, and the effect of everything that has passed through our body since that time.

At the same time, although every disorder has basic similarities, it may be found in different persons, thus there may be some unique aspects relative to that person's personal history. This is why the use of a certain herb may sometimes produce dramatic effects on one person's condition but have little effect on the same condition in another person.

In order to surmount this possible "weakness" in herbs, herbalists sometimes bring together a number of herbs which historically have been shown to affect the same organ or alleviate the same condition. With this "broad spectrum" approach, the probability of positive results is considerably increased.

The herbal combinations that follow are each made up of a number of herbs which work together to attain a positive result in alleviating the following conditions.

1. Combination for Gastro-intestinal Problems.
Proven helpful to relieve problems such as gastritis, heartburn, indigestion, colitis, colic and diverticulitis. It may be taken as tablets or tinctured drops.
Comfrey Leaf, Cayenne Pepper, Myrrh Gum, Peppermint

2. Combination for Internal Cleansing (Herbal Detoxification Formula)
Garlic, Chaparral, Foenugreek, Quassia, Red Sage, Black Cohosh, Golden Seal

3. Combination for Respiratory Ailments.

For deficiencies related to bronchitis, mucus and phlegm accumulation, chronic cough, pleurisy and asthma.

Slippery Elm, Thyme, Pleurisy Root, Comfrey, Yerba Santa

4. Combination for Female Complaints and Female Irregularities

A great help for amenorrehea, dysmenorrehea, cramps, discharge, and menopausal problems.

Red Raspberry, Damiana, Crampbark, Squaw Vine, Sarsaparilla, Black Cohosh, Licorice, Ginseng

5. Combination for Nervous Conditions and Relaxation

Valerian, Hops Flowers, Wood Betony, Chamomile, Scul-l cap, Passion Flower, Comfrey

6. Combination for Kidney Ailments

Alfalfa, Parsley, Uva Ursi, Corn Silk, Juniper, Buchu

7. Combination to Eliminate Parasites or Worms

Garlic, Black Walnut, Quassia, Mandrake

8. Combination to Regulate Blood Sugar Levels

Chaparral, Ginger, Blueberry Leaves, Dandelion Root, Golden Seal, Bilberry Leaves, Walnut Leaves

9. Combination to Reduce Fever

Blue Vervain, Comfrey, Buckthorn Bark, Chamomile, Cinchona Bark, Yarrow, Yarrow Flowers

10. Combination for Flu Symptoms

Yarrow, Chamomile, Pleurisy Root, Blessed Thistle, Catnip, Hyssop

11. Combination for Male Irregularities.
Excellent for relief of prostate problems.
Cayenne, Marshmallow, Golden Seal, Ginger, Juniper Berry

12. Combination to Depress the Appetite
Poke Root, Chickweed, Fennel

13. Combination to Strengthen the Heart and Circulatory System
Hawthorne Berry, Valerian, Peppermint, Passion Flower, Cayenne

14. Combination for Removing Mucus from The Small Intestine
Comfrey, Pepsin, Wheat Germ

Chapter 14

The Wonders of Clay

There is not a more fascinating and "down to earth" subject than clay, also known as mud or moorbad. Since before recorded history, clay was the standard treatment for many of mankind's ailments.

145

Digging Into the History

In Eastern and Western European countries mineral-rich mud treatments for the face and body have been accepted in medical practices and at resorts, spas, hospitals and clinics. The evidence of the benefits derived is overwhelming and the treatment is still popular in Europe today.

Years ago a certain trapper was frustrated when he got his sore, chapped hands covered with a white cheesy mud. Rather than washing in ice-cold water he waited until he returned home, there to find that his hands were not nearly as sore as before. After bringing home a can full of mud and applying it, his hands quickly healed and the skin stayed soft. Before long he found the mud helpful for scratches, wounds, sprains and burns. He thought that he had made a new discovery, but actually he had only rediscovered an age-old secret.

Uncovering the Secrets of Clay

How could something as "simple as mud" produce such dramatic results? If we really get into the "nitty gritty" of it, we'll find that it "ain't all dirt," but that there is some "solid ground" for these amazing results.

Consider the fact that clay contains 37 minerals and trace elements which enrich and revitalize new skin cells with a combination of essential elements that cannot be duplicated synthetically. Since it has a Ph factor of 6.5 to 7.3 it is naturally balanced and perfect for skin and hair.

Scientists have had to conclude that clay's properties are beyond the expected actions of the substances it contains. Several reasons for this have been put forward. First, seeing that clay can support life (as in the case of the shrimp which can live and grow in clay), it has been concluded that clay is a live medium which helps to generate and maintain life.

In addition, clay is known to have a negative electrical charge while toxic poisons have positive charges. This means that the poisons are drawn to and held by the clay. According to Dr. Robert T. Martin, a mineralogist at Massachusetts Institute of Technology, one gram of clay has a surface area of 800 square meters.

This enables it to attract and hold up to forty times its own weight in toxic poisons, thus cleansing and detoxifying.

The absorbent powers of clay were shown by Raymond Dextriet, a French Naturopath, who demonstrated that raw eggs covered with clay lost three times more weight than if they remained in the open air. This occured without any damage to the shell.

Dextriet found clay an effective antiseptic and antibiotic. Surprisingly he found that it does not act specifically on one particular type of bacteria, but rather prevents bacterial proliferation by reinforcing the natural defense mechanism.

Dr. Meyer-Camberg found that clay reduces the toxicity of harmful substances. He recommends clay for neutralizing poisons.

Laying It On — Practical Applications

Clay has many varied uses and it would be very difficult to list them all here, but I have listed some of the main ones. I would like to stress that clay applied externally should be accompanied by extra nutrients taken internally.

—Spread as a thick paste over *sores* or *burns* provides relief and healing

—A wet pack applied daily to a *boil* brought it to a head in three days.

— *Corns* and *calluses* on the toes and feet have been relieved in three to six days.

—A poultice on the body greatly increased *surface circulation*.

—*Ringworm* was cleared up by repeated applications.

—As a facial pack, clay cleared up *pimples,* leaving skin soft.

—*Eczema* treated by "everything" started clearing up in two days with the clay.

—Used as a powder it cleared up *diaper rash* overnight.

—Further reports confirm its usefulness in cases of *abscesses, arthritis, bruises, burns, cuts, hernias, varicose ulcers, rheumatism, cataracts, tonsillitis, sprains* and numerous other conditions.

Appendix A
Vitamin Reference Chart

Abbreviations

Acid — Acidophilus
Adren — Adrenal Stimulant
    Formula †
Cal — Calcium
Dig —Digestive Supplement †
FGlan — Female Multi Glandular †
Lec — Lecithin

MGlan — Male Multi Glandular†
Min — Chelated Multi Mineral†
Multi — Multi Vitamin Mineral †
PA — Pantothenic Acid
Pot — Potassium
Pro — Protein
Sel — Selenium

Acne	E, A, B6, PA, Zinc
Arteries	A, B6, C, E, Multi, Sel
Arthritis	B, C, E, Calcium, PA, Pro, Multi
Asthma	PA, C, A, E, Adren
Backache	C, Cal, Pro, Min
Bed Sores	B Complex
Blood Clotting	C, E, Cal,Min
— Inhibits Clotting	Pro, E, C, Lec, Multi
Blood Pressure	
— High	C, E, Multi, Lec, Sel, Pot
— Low	B, C, E, PA, Pro, Sel
Bruising	C
Burns	B, C, E
Canker Sores	B6, Niacin, B
Cholesterol	A. B6, C, E,Lec, Multi
Cold Sores	PA, C, B6
Colds	PA, C, B, Min
Colitis	Multi, PA, Min
Constipation	Multi, B, E, PA
Diarrhea	B6, B, Niacin,Multi, Pot
Digestion	Acid, Dig, A, B, C, E, Lec

Eczema	Niacin, B, B6, Multi
Eyes	A, C, E, PA, B, Pro
Fingernails	Pro, A, Cal
Flu	C, E, B6, B, Multi
Gout	B, C, E, PA, Min
Hair	Pro, B, Multi, Zinc
Kidney Stones	Cal, B6, Min, C
Liver	Pro, A,C,E,B,Min
Motion Sickness	B6, B
Muscular Cramps	B6, Cal, PA, Multi, Adren
Nervousness	B, Cal, Min, B6
Nosebleeds	C
Ovaries	C, Min, Fe Glan
Prostate	A, C, Min, Zinc, MGlan
Psoriasis	B6, Lec, A
Sinus	A, B6, C, E, PA
Stretch Marks	E, PA
Throat, Sore	C, B
Ulcers	A, B, C, E, PA
Varicose Veins	B, C, E, Lec, Min
Warts	A, E
Wrinkles	B6, E, A

Appendix B
Herb Reference Chart

(See also Chapter 13: Herbal Combinations)

Acne   Barley Green, Bee Pollen, Chaparral,
                Yellow Dock
Adrenal Glands Licorice Root
Aging   Bee Pollen, Ginseng, Gotu Kola
Allergies   Barley Green, Bee Pollen, Spirulina,
Anemia   Alfalfa, Comfrey, Dandelion,Spirulina, Yellow
                Dock
Appetite Depresant   Chickweed,
Arthritis   Alfalfa, Barley Green, Capsicum, Chaparral,
                Poke Root,Sarsaparilla, Yucca
Asthma   Black Cohosh, Lobelia, Mullein, Thyme
Atherosclerosis Hawthorne Berry
Bladder   Alfalfa, Horsetail,Uva Ursi
Blood — oxygenation   Black Walnut Leaves
    — purifier Chaparral, Dandelion, Echinacea, Poke
                Root, Sarsaparilla, Yellow Dock, Yucca
Blood Pressure
    — high   Barley Green, Dandelion, Garlic, Hawthorne
                Berry, Evening Primrose
Blood Pressure — low   Hawthorn Berry
Blood Sugar — balance   Black Walnut Leaves,
Blood Sugar — low   Hawthorne Berry, Licorice Root
Bones, broken   Comfrey, Horsetail
Bronchials   Chamomile,Comfrey, Ginger, Lobelia, Thyme
Chemotherapy   Spirulina
Childbirth   Black Cohosh,
Circulation   Capsicum, Ginger
Colds   Capsicum, Garlic, Ginger, Licorice Root,
                Safflower, Golden Seal
Colic   Chamomile, Wood Betony
Constipation   Cascara Sagrada,
Coughs   Ginger, Licorice Root, Lobelia, Thyme
Cramps — stomach   Barley Green, Black Walnut Leaves,
                Ginger, Wood Betony

Diabetes	Dandelion , Golden Seal, Spirulina, Uva Ursi
Diarrhea	Mullein, Thyme, White Oak Bark
Digestive Disorders	Alfalfa, Barley Green, Bee Pollen, Garlic, Wood Betony
Drug WIthdrawal	Chamomile,
Drugs, Resistance to	Ginseng
Ears	Chickweed, Garlic, Lobelia, Yellow Dock
Eyes	Eyebright, Spirulina
Fatigue	Bee Pollen, Garlic, Ginseng, Gotu Kola,
Female Complaints	Black Cohosh, Damiana, Licorice , Uva Ursi
Female Hormone Imbalance	Damiana, Sarsaparilla
Fever	Chamomile, Safflower
Flu	Capsicum, Ginger
Gallbladder	Safflower, Cascara Sagrada
Gas	Ginger, Sarsaparilla, Thyme
Hair, Nails, Teeth	Horsetail
Headache	Ginger, Thyme, White Willow , Wood Betony
Heart	Capsicum, Hawthorne Berry, Mullein,
Hemmorrhoids	Mullein, White Oak Bark
Hypoglycemia	see Blood Sugar — Low
Impotency	see Sexual Debility
Infection	Echinacea, Garlic, Golden Seal
Insomnia	Chamomile, Valerian
Intestinal Tract — Inflamation	Licorice Root
Kidney	Alfalfa, Barley Green, Capsicum, Horsetail, Uva Ursa
Lead removal	Barley Green, Spirulina
Liver	Barley Green, Chaparral, Dandelion Safflower, Spirulina, Yellow Dock
Lungs	Chickweed, Lobelia, Mullein
Lymphatics	Chaparral,
Membranes — inflamation	Chickweed, Comfrey, Golden Seal,
Menstrual Pain	Black Cohosh, White Oak Bark

Menstrual Flow	
— excessive	Uva Ursi
— stimulation	Chamomile, Thyme
Mercury removal	Barley Green, Spirulina
Motion Sicknes	Ginger,
Muscles — Cramps	Safflower
— Spasms	Valerian
Nervous Disorders	Chamomile, Gotu Kola, Thyme, Valerian, Wood Betony
Obesity	Chickweed, Kelp, Poke Root
Pain	Mullein, Valerian, White Willow Bark
Pancreas	Dandelion, Spirulina, Uva Ursi
Parasites	Black Walnut Leaves, Garlic, Sarsaparilla, Wood Betony
Poison, Resistance to	Barley Green, Ginseng, Sarsaparilla,
Prostate disease	Bee Pollen, Echinacea, Kelp
Psoriasis	Dandelion, Sarsaparilla, Yellow Dock
Radiation	Ginseng, Spirulina
Respiratory	Comfrey, Lobelia, Mullein,
Rheumatism	Capsicum, Poke Root, Sarsaparilla, Yucca
Senility	Gotu Kola
Sexual Debility	Bee Pollen, Damiana, Licorice Root, Ginseng
Skin	Horsetail, Sarsaparilla, Yellow Dock, Yucca
Spleen	Dandelion , Poke Root, Uva Ursi
Stimulant	Capsicum,
Stomach — upset	Chamomile, Ginger
Stress	Lobelia,
Throats, sore	Bee Pollen, Garlic, Ginger, Licorice, WhiteOak
Thyroid	Kelp, Poke Root
Tumors	Chaparral, Chickweed, Echinacea, Yellow Dock
Ulcers	Capsicum, Licorice, Spirulina, Yellow Dock
Urethral Tract	Chaparral, Uva Ursi
Varicose Veins	Black Walnut, Capsicum, White Oak Bark
Viral Infections	Echinacea,Safflower, Uva Urs

Appendix C
Master Formulas

Adrenal Stimulant Formula

Potassium	100 mg
Pantothenic Acid	100 mg
Vitamin B6	5 mg
Adrenal Substance	20 mg
Licorice	5 mg

Digestive Enzyme Supplement

Papain	65 mg
Pepsin	30 mg
Whole Bile Salts	65 mg
Pancreatin	10 mg
Betaine Hydrochloride	105 mg

Herbal Detoxification Formula

Garlic, Chaparral, Feoenugreek, Quassia, Black Cohosh, Red Sage, Golden Seal.

Herbal Intestinal Cleanse Formula

Comfrey Root, Wheat Germ, Pepsin

Female Multi Glandular

Ovarian Substance, Adrenal Substance, Thymus Substance, Pancreas Substance, Kidney Substance, Heart Substance, Kelp, RNA, Pituitary Substance.

Male Multi Glandular

Prostate Substance, Adrenal Substance, Thymus Substance, Pancreas Substance, Kidney Substance, Heart Substance, RNA, Pituitary Substance, Kelp.

Multi Vitamin Mineral

Vitamin A	4165 IU
D	135 IU
C	200 mg
B1	10 mg
B2	10 mg
B6	10 mg
B12	15 mcg
E	65 IU
Niacin	5 mg
Niacinamide	5 mg
Pantothenic Acid	15 mg
Folic Acid	.066 mg
Biotin	15 mcg
Calcium	165 mg
Magnesium	65 mg
Potassium	15 mg
Iron	2.5 mg
Iodine	37 mg
Chromium	15 mcg
Manganese	2.5 mg
Zinc	2.5 mg
Selenium	15 mcg
Betaine HCl	25 mg
PABA	10 mg
Choline	10 mg
Inositol	10 mg

Chelated Multi Minerals

Calcium	50 mg	Chromium	15 mg
Phosphorus	50 mg	Potassium	30 mg
Iron	5 mg	Manganese	10 mg
Magnesium	25 mg	Iodine	.075 mg
Copper	1 mg	Selenium	.065 mg
Zinc	5 mg		

Appendix D
Suggested Readings and Bibliography

Abehsera, Michel. *The Healing Clay.* Secaucus, NJ: Citadel Press, 1977

Beebe, Rupert. *Candida Yeast Infection.* Surrey, BC: Healthology, 1988

Black, Dean, Ph.D. *Health at the Crossroads.* Springville, VT: Tapestry Press, 1988

Cheraskin, E.; W.M. Ringsdorf; and I.W. Clark. *Diet and Disease.* New Canaan, CT: Keats Publishing, 1968

Crook, William G., M.D. *The Yeast Connection.* Jackson, TN: Professional Books, 1986

Fisher, Greg Charles; and Stephen E. Strauss, M.D. *Chronic Fatigue Syndrome.* New York: Warner Books, 1989

Jensen, Bernard, D.C. *Tissue Cleansing Through Bowel Management.* Escondido, CA: 1981

Heinerman, John. *Herbal Dynamics.* Root of Life Inc.,1982

Hutchens, Alma R. *Indian Herbology of North America.* Windsor, ON: 1973

Lust, John B., N.D. *The Herb Book.* New York: Bantam Books, 1974

Philpott, William H., and Dwight K. Kaleta, Ph.D. *Brain Allergies.* New Canaan, CT: Keats Publishing, 1980

Potts, Eve, and Marion Morra. *Understanding Your Immune System.* New York: Avon Books, 1986

Rowland, David, Ph.D., R.N.C. *Vascular Cleansing: New Hope for Heart Disease.* Uxbridge, ON: 1986

Stoff, Jesse A., and Charles Pellegrino. *Chronic Fatigue Syndrome.* New York: Random House 1988

Tenny, Louise. *Today's Herbal Health.* Provo UT: Woodland Books 1983

Thomson, William, A.R., M.D. *Medicine from the Earth.* New York: McGraw Hill 1978

Trowbridge, John Parks, M.D. and Morton Walker, D.P.M. *The Yeast Syndrome.* New York: Bantam Books 1986

Truss, C. Orian, M.D., *The Missing Diagnosis.* Birmingham, AL: Missing Diagnos Inc. 1983

Walker, Norman W., D.Sc., Ph.D. *Colon Health: The Key to Vibrant Health.* Prescott, AZ: 1979